DUBLIN & WICKLOW
A WALKING GUIDE

HELEN FAIRBAIRN is a full-time travel writer and has written numerous walking guidebooks, exploring destinations as diverse as America's Rocky Mountains, the European Alps and Scotland's highlands and islands. A regular contributor to *Walking World Ireland* magazine, Helen has spent years researching the best walking routes in Ireland. Her other walking guides for The Collins Press are *Ireland's Best Walks*, *Ireland's Wild Atlantic Way* and *Northern Ireland*.

The photographs in this book are the work of Irish landscape photographer **GARETH McCORMACK**, author of *The Mountains of Ireland*. For more information or to license the images, see www.garethmccormack.com.

The view north across Killiney Bay from the 197m summit of Bray Head.

Acknowledgements

Many thanks to those who accompanied me on research trips for this guide, including Aaron, Erin, Geordan, Ken, Mohammad, Des and Tom. Thanks to Gary, Eadoin, Dave and Dee for their wonderful hospitality. And, most of all, thanks to Gareth for extended company and support work, and to Dermot for holding the fort at home while I headed off into the wild.

Advice to Readers

Every effort is made by our authors to ensure the accuracy of our guidebooks. However, changes can occur after a book has been printed. If you notice discrepancies between this guidebook and the facts on the ground, please let us know, either by email to enquiries@collinspress.ie or by post to The Collins Press, West Link Park, Doughcloyne, Wilton, Cork, T12 N5EF, Ireland.

A walker on the coastal path near Red Rock, on the southern side of the Howth peninsula, County Dublin.

DUBLIN & WICKLOW
A WALKING GUIDE

HELEN FAIRBAIRN

The
Collins
Press

First published in 2014 by
The Collins Press
West Link Park
Doughcloyne
Wilton
Cork

Reprinted 2015, 2017

Paperback ISBN: 978-1-84889-201-9

Design and typesetting by Fairways Design
Typeset in Myriad Pro
Printed in Poland by Białostockie Zakłady Graficzne SA

Contents

Route Location Map

Quick Reference Route Table

No.	Walk Name	Category
1 ✓	Howth Cliff Path	Coastal Path
2	Fairy Castle Loop	Forest and Mountain Trail
3 ✓	Bray Head	Coastal Path
4	Prince William's Seat	Forest Trail and Hillwalk
5	Wicklow Way Day 1 – Marlay Park to Knockree	Road, Forest and Mountain Trail
6	Wicklow Way Day 2 – Knockree to Roundwood	Forest and Mountain Trail
7	Wicklow Way Day 3 – Roundwood to Glendalough	Road, Forest and Mountain Trail
8	Wicklow Way Day 4 – Glendalough to Glenmalure	Forest and Mountain Trail
9	Seefingan Circuit	Hillwalk
10	Kippure and the two Lough Brays	Hillwalk
11 ✓	Maulin Circuit	Forest Trail and Hillwalk
12	Powerscourt Waterfall from Crone	Road and Forest Trail
13	Great Sugar Loaf – Out and Back from the South	Mountain Trail
	Great Sugar Loaf – Circuit from the East	Mountain Trail
14	Djouce and War Hill	Hillwalk
15	Mullaghcleevaun from the North	Hillwalk
16	Mullaghcleevaun from the South	Hillwalk
17	Luggala and Knocknacloghoge	Hillwalk
18	Tonelagee	Hillwalk
19	Scarr and Kanturk	Hillwalk
20	The Devil's Glen	Woodland Trail
21	Kilcoole Coastal Path	Coastal Path
22	Camaderry Circuit	Hillwalk
23 ✓	The Spinc Loop	Mountain Trail
24	Mullacor Circuit	Hillwalk
25	Vale of Clara	Woodland Trail
26	Lugnaquilla from the Glen of Imaal	Hillwalk
27	Lugnaquilla from Glenmalure	Hillwalk
28	Lugnaquilla via the South Prison	Hillwalk

Grade	Distance	Ascent	Time	Page
2	10km	240m	3–3½ hours	11
2	6km	230m	1½–2½ hours	16
2	10km	290m	3–3½ hours	20
3	10.5km	400m	3–4 hours	24
3	21km	650m	6–7 hours	30
3	21km	690m	6–7 hours	34
3	13km	360m	3½–4 hours	39
3	14km	450m	4–5 hours	43
4	10km	560m	3½–4 hours	47
4	7.5km	350m	2½–3½ hours	52
3	7km	420m	2½–3½ hours	56
2	6.5km	260m	2–2½ hours	60
3	3km	210m	1–1¼ hours	63
3	5km	380m	2–2½ hours	66
4	14km	660m	4½–5½ hours	68
4	12km	630m	4–5 hours	72
4	8.5km	570m	3–3½ hours	76
5	12km	780m	4½–5½ hours	80
4	8km	490m	3–4 hours	85
4	14km	540m	4–5 hours	89
1	5km	130m	1½ hours	93
1	14km	30m	3–4 hours	96
4	13km	630m	4–5 hours	100
3	11.5km	400m	3½–4 hours	105
4	11.5km	640m	4–5 hours	109
2	9.5km	100m	2½–3 hours	114
5	19km	920m	6½–7½ hours	120
5	13km	800m	5–6 hours	125
5	16km	735m	5–6 hours	130

View along the Cloghoge valley, County Wicklow.

Walking in Dublin and Wicklow: An Introduction

At first glance, Dublin and Wicklow seem like counties that are diametrically opposed. Dublin is synonymous with the thriving urban metropolis that is Ireland's capital city, while Wicklow is known as the Garden of Ireland, and contains the largest contiguous mountain area in the country.

The reality of course is that the geographical boundaries between the two counties are not as defined as they might seem. In fact the Dublin and Wicklow Mountains form part of the same, continuous range, and extend right down to the southern suburbs of the capital. The coastline is even more dispersed – from a stretch of shoreline over 120km long, the wildest coastal terrain can actually be found guarding either side of Dublin Bay.

The truth is that both counties offer some fine hillwalking, as well as a diverse range of lowland routes. From woodland trails and scenic coastal paths, to challenging ascents and wild mountain summits, there are some fantastic routes here for walkers of all persuasions.

In deciding which routes to include in this guide, I have concentrated on exploring the region's wild, natural landforms. These vary from dramatic corries and sheer cliffs, to secluded lakes and verdant forests. Some of the routes are established classics, while others focus on hidden gems that are more off the beaten track. The common thread is that all of these landscapes are away from roads, and can only be explored on foot.

My hope is that you will find the routes as satisfying as I do. Most are readily accessible and can be reached within an hour of Dublin city, so there is little to stop you getting out there to judge for yourself. Walking energises the mind and body, and discovering new landscapes leads to a better appreciation of the natural world. So why not pick your route, select a fine, sunny day, and head out? I hope you enjoy the journey.

Landscape

The neighbouring counties of Dublin and Wicklow have a combined area of almost 3,000 square kilometres. Dublin is the most heavily populated county in Ireland with 1,380 people per square kilometre, compared with just sixty-seven people who live in the same area in County Wicklow. Yet there are large parts of both counties that are barely populated at all. In fact Wicklow contains the largest swathe of mountainous upland in Ireland, and it is quite possible to drive across the hills for 30km or more and pass hardly a single house.

The mountains themselves include over 500 square kilometres above 300m high. Within this area there thirty-nine summits that reach over

600m high, with the tallest point – at the top of Lugnaquilla – extending to 925m. One of the most significant factors that helped to shape these peaks was the last Ice Age. The region has countless fine examples of post-glacial topography, including deep valleys, chiselled corries and upland lakes, as well as oddly placed glacial erratics left behind by the retreating ice.

The range is formed predominately of granite and is part of a huge expanse of rock that extends all the way from Dublin to Wexford, making this the largest granite mass in Europe outside Russia's Ural Mountains. The bedrock is visible only in isolated areas, however. More often it lies hidden beneath a thick blanket of peat bog, which has been accumulating in some places for up to 4,000 years and is considered an endangered habitat by international standards.

Many lower slopes are also covered by great swathes of pine forest. Millennia of human-led deforestation meant that by 1800 Ireland was the least-forested country in Europe. Though pockets of genuinely native, deciduous woodland are now extremely rare, the state's twentieth-century forestry policy means that managed pine plantations are widespread. Planting activity was particularly extensive in Wicklow and 17 per cent of the county is now covered in trees, making this the most forested county in Ireland.

The mountains of Dublin and Wicklow are also one of the best places in Ireland to see large wild animals. The most visible creatures are the deer, which you have a high chance of seeing on any of the upland routes in this book. These beasts are all descendants of two herds that were reintroduced to the Powerscourt estate in the eighteenth century, after the native red deer had been hunted to extinction. They are either pure sika deer, or hybrid sika-red deer. Other creatures you may see on your travels include feral goats, hares, lizards and frogs.

Many of the region's best natural landscapes are now protected within different parks and reserves. The largest of these is Wicklow Mountains National Park, which was established in 1991. At the time of writing this encompasses some 200 square kilometres of mountain upland and wooded valleys, making it the largest national park in Ireland. The boundaries are likely to expand further too, thanks to an ongoing policy of acquiring suitable ground as it is put up for sale. Along with numerous smaller reserves and special conservation areas, this provides a reassuring level of protection to help preserve the region's natural assets into the future.

Walking Practicalities

The fantastically varied landscapes of Dublin and Wicklow offer a host of exciting itineraries for walkers. But there are some challenges too. Prime amongst these is devising an itinerary that minimises the amount of time spent crossing the open bog.

As you follow the Military Road across the top of the Wicklow uplands, it is hard not to be impressed by the sheer mass of peat bog surrounding you. This habitat may be ecologically precious, but it also provides an extremely arduous walking surface. The routes highlighted here have been designed to minimise the amount of bog-trotting, and concentrate instead on exploring the region's most dramatic landforms via the most direct and rewarding routes possible.

One of the consequences of being so close to the capital is the ready supply of walkers who want to explore the region. Wicklow has long been considered Dublin's outdoor playground, and this is not a destination where you should expect solitude. Places like Glendalough and Glenmacnass overflow with all the colours of humanity on summer weekends, while the routes around Great Sugar Loaf and Bray Head are popular with local walkers all year round. That is not to suggest that isolation is impossible – pick one of the routes off the beaten track, especially in winter, and there is a high likelihood you will not see another soul on your travels.

The region's popularity has many positive implications for walkers too. Walking routes tend to be long-established, and access disputes are relatively rare. This is helped by the existence of such a large national park, whose regulations specifically guarantee open access for walkers.

Access is also relatively simple in terms of reaching the start of the walks. Most of the routes around the city can be reached quickly and easily using the city's public transport network. Further south, away from the city, there is quick, convenient road access to most of the region's highest peaks. There are also plenty of backcountry car parks, and you will generally be able to park easily near the start of your chosen route.

Unfortunately, however, theft from parked cars is a problem. There were 254 reported thefts from vehicles in Wicklow in the three months of June, July and August 2013 alone. Walkers are advised to hide all belongings out of sight before they leave their car, and to report all thefts and suspicious activity to the Gardaí.

The good network of roads means many of the hill-walks start fairly high up, and have a relatively modest total ascent of around 600m. The one exception is Lugnaquilla, which is so high, and whose surrounding valleys are so deep, it is hard reach the summit without at least 800m of ascent. This is just one of the ways in which Lugnaquilla is in a class of its own, and I make no apologies for describing three different routes up its flanks.

The region's high footfall has led to the formation of paths in many mountain areas. This is a big help in terms of navigation, but it does have environmental implications in terms of erosion and visual scarring. National Park staff work in partnership with volunteer groups like Mountain Meitheal to minimise the impact on the landscape by building trails and undertaking restoration work in the most popular walking areas.

3

Despite the existence of constructed and informal paths, you will still need to be self-reliant in terms of navigation to venture into these hills in safety. You will need to carry a map and compass on all upland routes, and know how to use them. In bad weather in particular, solid navigational skills are a prerequisite for completing these hill-walks in safety.

If you are concerned about the navigational challenges of hillwalking, it may be advisable to stick to the region's signed routes. Dublin and Wicklow have a wide range of marked walking trails, the best of which are also included in this book. These routes generally follow formal tracks and footpaths, and are signposted throughout. The longest, best-established trail is the Wicklow Way, the first half of which is described in this guide.

A Wicklow Walking Odyssey

As well as offering a host of great one-day trips, Wicklow is one of the best places in Ireland to link routes together into a longer walking adventure. Many longer itineraries use the Wicklow Way to link circuits together, and it is quite possible to spend ten days or more exploring some of the best peaks in Wicklow while barely resorting to motorised transport at all. The itinerary suggested below is just one of many possibilities.

Day 1 – Wicklow Way Day 1 (see p. 30). Include detours to the summits of Fairy Castle and Prince William's Seat. Stay at Knockree Youth Hostel.

Day 2 – Wicklow Way Day 2 (see p. 34). Include a detour to the summit of Djouce, and stay in Roundwood.

Day 3 – Taxi from Roundwood to the Pier Gates above Lough Tay. Complete the Luggala & Knocknacloghoge circuit (see p. 80), but finish by crossing the Inchavore River and following the track around the northeast base of Kanturk. Stay in Lough Dann House, Oldbridge.

Day 4 – Scarr and Kanturk circuit (see p. 89), but finish by following Wicklow Way Day 3 (see p. 39) to Glendalough. Stay in Glendalough Youth Hostel.

Day 5 – Spinc Loop (see p. 105).

Day 6 – Camaderry Circuit (see p. 100).

Day 7 – Wicklow Way Day 4 from Glendalough to Glenmalure (see p. 43). Stay in Glenmalure Youth Hostel.

Day 8 – Complete your odyssey with the fabulous Lugnaquilla from Glenmalure (see p. 125).

Climate

Dublin and Wicklow enjoy a relatively mild climate all year round, with the prevailing winds coming from the west or southwest. Ashford Weather Station, 5km north of Wicklow town, records an average of 129 days of precipitation each year. Although the winter is wetter, there are still ten days of rain during most of the summer months. The moral is that it is advisable to be prepared for showers even on apparently sunny days.

Prolonged spells of wet weather saturate the upland peat, making walking conditions boggy and arduous underfoot. In these conditions, it is best to wear gaiters and avoid routes that cross a lot of open moorland. Rainfall also affects the water levels; mountain streams that might normally be a trickle can be transformed into raging torrents after a few hours of heavy rain. River crossings can be very dangerous in spate conditions, and you should consider the effect of different water levels when planning your route.

The warmest months are July and August, with average temperatures of 11°C to 21°C. However, many of the best outdoor experiences can be had on crisp, clear days in autumn, winter or spring. The coldest months are January and February, when daytime temperatures vary from 2°C to 9°C, and night-time temperatures often drop below freezing. This is enough to freeze upland bog, and it is a great time to tackle the region's wetter walking routes. It is wonderful to skip across frozen peat, knowing you might be sinking knee-deep at other times.

Lowland areas rarely have more than a few days' snow each year. In the mountains, snow is more frequent and may linger for a week or more on the summits. It can cover paths, cairns and other navigational aids, and turn even moderately steep slopes into hazardous slides, so make sure you have the experience and equipment to cope with the conditions. Mountain access roads are often closed after heavy snowfalls too – especially around the Sally Gap and Wicklow Gap – so check the road conditions as well as the weather forecast before heading out in the winter.

Wind chill is perhaps the biggest danger to winter walkers once they are out in the elements. As a rule the air temperature drops 2–3°C for every 300m of height gained. Add even a moderate wind-chill factor and it soon becomes obvious that several layers of insulation might be needed to keep warm.

Another seasonal consideration for walkers is the amount of daylight. In mid-December the sun rises around 8.40 a.m. and sets soon after 4 p.m., giving just seven and a half hours of daylight. By mid June, the sun does not set until 10 p.m. and there are seventeen hours of daylight. It is quite possible to start an eight-hour walk at lunchtime and still finish with daylight to spare.

Maps

Dublin and Wicklow have the widest choice of outdoor mapping in Ireland, and there is a range of good maps to choose from.

The long-established, standard reference for Irish walkers is the Ordnance Survey of Ireland (OSi) 1:50,000 *Discovery* series. This series covers the whole country; sheets 50, 56 and 62 are the relevant ones for the routes in this book. Sheet 56 is also available with a waterproof covering. The general quality and accuracy of the mapping is very high, though it tends to lack detail in the placement of forest tracks and mountain paths.

The region's most popular walking areas are also covered by smaller-scale mapping. The 1:30,000 Harvey Superwalker map, *Wicklow Mountains*, is waterproof, detailed and shows many paths and tracks better than the OSi equivalent. It depicts only the area covered by the Wicklow Mountains National Park. EastWest Mapping also offer four water-resistant, 1:30,000 maps that cover all of the Dublin and Wicklow Mountains. Their portrayal of forestry tracks and upland paths is certainly the most accurate and detailed of all the maps available, and many local walkers have found themselves switching to this series from the OSi equivalent.

It is worth noting that there are often small discrepancies between the different maps, particularly in the spelling of place names and height of mountains. I have generally used the standard OSi references unless there is good reason to do otherwise.

Useful Contacts

Listed below are the contact details of various service providers that might be of assistance to walkers.

Emergencies Dial 999 or 112 for all emergency services, including mountain rescue and coastguard.

Weather The Irish Meteorological Service provides a two-day online weather forecast for Ireland at www.met.ie. A five-day telephone forecast for Leinster is also available from Met Éireann's Weatherdial service on Tel: 1550 123 851.

Maps To purchase walking maps from outside the region, go to the online shops at www.osi.ie, www.harveymaps.co.uk, or www.eastwestmapping.ie.

Wicklow Mountains National Park For more information on the park, its history, landscape, regulations and walking trails, contact Tel: 0404 45425; www.wicklowmountainsnationalpark.ie.

Forest Service The managed forestry plantations in Ireland are overseen by Coillte, the semi-state forestry company. For more information about the facilities and walking trails in each forest, see www.coillteoutdoors.ie.

Hillwalking Resource A great resource for walkers is: www.mountainviews. ie. This website provides practical details about all Ireland's mountains, with walkers' comments detailing different routes up each peak.

The Wicklow Way For a host of practical and background information on this renowned long-distance walking trail, see www.wicklowway.com.

Transport Bus services in and around Dublin city are run by Dublin Bus. For full timetable information, contact Tel: 01 873 4222; www.dublinbus.ie. For DART rail services, contact Tel: 01 703 3504; www.irishrail.ie/DART. For intercity train services, contact Irish Rail on Tel: 1850 366 222; www.irishrail. ie. For intercity bus services, contact Bus Éireann on Tel: 01 836 6111; www. buseireann.ie.

Tourist Information Tourist Information for Dublin city is available from the Dublin Discover Ireland Centre, 14 Upper O Connell Street, Tel: 01 605 7700; www.visitdublin.com. For information concerning County Wicklow, contact Tel: 0404 200 70; www.visitwicklow.ie.

Using This Guide

This guide consists of twenty-eight route descriptions for one-day walks in Dublin and Wicklow. All the routes were checked in 2013, and descriptions were correct at that time.

Many of the walks around Dublin and Glendalough are accessible by public transport, but you will need your own vehicle to reach the more remote excursions. The majority of the routes are circular in format, though there are also a few linear itineraries that use public transport to return to the starting point.

The guide offers a wide variety of route options to suit every sort of walker. Many of the routes are hill-walks, but these range from relatively short, signed loops to challenging trips across the open summits. The remainder of the outings are lower woodland or coastal excursions. Many of the descriptions include suggestions for extending the route, and some of the days – like the sections of the Wicklow Way – can also be walked consecutively to make a multi-day excursion.

Virtually all the walking takes place across open ground or along footpaths and tracks. Road walking has been kept to a bare minimum, and main roads have been avoided altogether.

Grading

Grades have been included to give an indication of the overall difficulty level, 1 being the easiest and 5 the hardest. None of the routes involves any technical difficulties that require rock-climbing skills.

Grade 1   Relatively short walks on well-graded paths. Surfaces are largely firm underfoot and little ascent or descent is involved. Routes are generally signposted. No serious navigational difficulties.

Grade 2   Routes still follow paths, but these might not be maintained or signposted. Some sections may cross rougher ground or open countryside. There are no sustained ascents or descents, and no serious navigational difficulties.

Grade 3   Walks in this category may involve a significant amount of vertical ascent, and take more than four hours to complete. Terrain can be rough underfoot, though formal paths may still exist. Navigation skills are required but route finding should be relatively straightforward in good conditions. Most of the region's easy hill-walks and the long-distance Wicklow Way fall into this category.

Grade 4   Longer mountain excursions with up to 700m of vertical ascent. Ground can be very rough underfoot and any paths are informal in character. Navigational skills are required throughout and may be necessary to avoid natural hazards such as cliffs. Previous hillwalking experience is required.

Grade 5   The longest, most strenuous hill-walks fall into this category. Routes generally visit multiple summits, last at least five hours and involve up to 1,000m of ascent. Good stamina, solid navigational skills, and previous hillwalking experience are all pre-requisites to complete the route in safety.

Sketch Maps

Each walk description is accompanied by a sketch map, to help you locate the route on the relevant reference map. The major features of the landscape are marked, along with any smaller points that may help you follow the route. Please note that scales and bearings are indicative rather than precise, and sketch maps should not be relied on for navigational purposes.

Equipment

Boots are required for all walks unless the route description advises otherwise. Another general rule of walking in Ireland is that you should always be prepared for adverse weather. In the mountains in particular, warm and waterproof clothing is essential even on an apparently sunny day. Gaiters are advisable for cross-country routes after rain.

It is also assumed that the relevant map sheet and a compass will be carried on all routes. Mobile phone coverage is generally good on high ground in the region, but may be less reliable in remote valleys. Do not rely on being able to get a connection whenever you need it.

Responsible Walking

Some of the walking routes described in this book depend on the goodwill of landowners for their existence. Inconsiderate behaviour by walkers may lead to access being withdrawn and apparently established routes being lost. Damage to farm fences and walls, sheep-worrying dogs and litter are some of the main reasons why walkers become unpopular with landowners.

Inconsiderate outdoor behaviour can also have a negative impact on the environment and on other people's enjoyment of the area. Leave No Trace Ireland is a network of organisations that promote responsible recreational use of the outdoors. They have designed a programme to help outdoor enthusiasts understand the impact of their activities and to value the natural environment. For full details of the principles involved, please see www.leavenotraceireland.org

Looking over Lough Tay to the cliffs of Luggala, County Wicklow.

Feral goat in the upper Glendalough valley, County Wicklow.

Very good Felo 2019

Howth Cliff Path

A signed path leads you past the dramatic cliffs and surprisingly wild coastline of the Howth peninsula, just a stone's throw from Dublin city.

Grade:	2
Time:	3–3½ hours
Distance:	10km (6 miles)
Ascent:	240m (790ft)
Map:	OSi 1:50,000 sheet 50

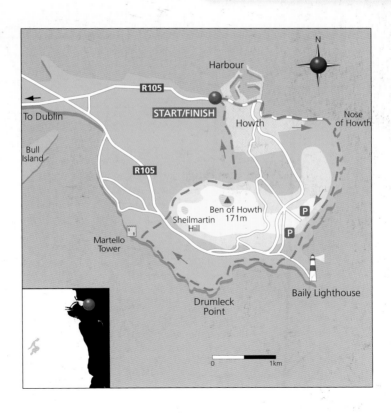

11

Heading towards the Baily Lighthouse on the eastern side of the peninsula.

Start & Finish: Howth DART station (grid ref: O282394). There are regular DART services from here to central Dublin and Greystones, and connections can be made onto Irish Rail's intercity network. If you are arriving in Howth by car, park in the large car park between the DART station and the harbour.

Though the coastline around much of Dublin Bay is predictably urban, it is enclosed to the north and south by headlands that are surprisingly wild in character. The Howth peninsula, on the northern side of the city, boasts a 3km-long cliff-line whose rugged and untamed nature would seem more at home on Ireland's western seaboard than alongside the country's largest metropolis.

The dramatic coastal terrain is offset by the area's wonderful scenery. During the summer, patches of pink thrift and yellow gorse line the path, and on a clear day the views stretch from the serrated skyline of Wicklow to Northern Ireland's Mourne Mountains. During the breeding season the skies teem with activity too – Howth holds the largest seabird colony on Ireland's east coast, and the offshore outcrops of Ireland's Eye and Lambay Island support bird populations of international importance.

In recent years the headland's trails have been organised into a series of looped walks, and this route follows the longest trail. Known as the Bog of Frogs Loop, the circuit is signed throughout by purple arrows. Landmarks along the way include Baily Lighthouse, and there is an optional detour to the summit of the 171m-high Ben of Howth.

12

Stiles and steps are in place to aid your progress wherever necessary, but much of the path remains distinctly wild so boots are definitely required. Note too that some sections of the trail pass along the top of steep cliffs, so you should avoid walking in windy conditions.

The Walk

From Howth DART station, turn east and follow the purple arrows along the pavement. Cross a road and join a wide promenade that leads pleasantly around the back of the harbour. This was constructed in 1812 to receive passengers from England, though it is overshadowed today by the adjacent marina, which is mainly used as a mooring spot for yachts and other pleasure craft.

When the promenade ends, bear right and follow Balscadden Road around the coast. At the bottom of this road on the right you will notice a Martello tower, one of a series of lookout posts built during the Napoleonic Wars to protect the Irish coast from French invasion. The road climbs gently past Balscadden House, home to the poet W. B. Yeats between 1880 and 1883. The tarmac soon comes to an end at a car park, and the cliff path continues ahead. The trail is well-trodden and obvious underfoot as it makes its way up the rough coastal slope. Already there is a good sense of wilderness in your surroundings, with fine views extending north over Lambay Island and the precipitous outcrop of Ireland's Eye.

Descending steps in the cliff at Red Rock, on the southern side of the peninsula.

On the coastal path near Red Rock, on the southern side of the peninsula.

Pass around the Nose of Howth, following the path as it sweeps south. You can now settle back and enjoy 2.5km of fine, uninterrupted coastal walking along this wild headland. Between April and August the cliffs are alive with the bustle of nesting seabirds, and soon Baily Lighthouse comes into view, perched at the end of a promontory on the southeastern tip of the peninsula.

Continue to a path junction; three shorter walking trails are signed off to the right here, but you should continue straight ahead, still following the purple arrows. The path begins to descend now, passing a house and dropping down to the lighthouse access road. There has been a lighthouse here since the mid 1600s but the present structure was built in 1814, and was the last lighthouse in Ireland to be automated.

Cross straight over the road, following a narrow path around the back of a house. The trail traces the southern coast of the peninsula for another 3km, running along the top of low cliffs beneath a series of houses.

The best views are now southward across Dublin Bay to the Wicklow Mountains. Once you have passed Drumleck Point the trail descends to the shore itself, climbing up and down across a series of rocky coves. The next challenge is a flight of steps that has been cut into the rock, with handholds in place for safety.

A second Martello tower now comes into sight ahead. Continue to a path junction around 250m east of the tower, then turn right. Climb inland to a grassy meadow, where you should follow the signs left, then right. This brings you to a road, which you cross straight over. The next part of the walk climbs across the eastern slopes of Sheilmartin Hill. The trail is bordered by bracken and gorse, and as you gain height there are good views northwest over the sandy isthmus that connects Howth to the mainland.

You now arrive at Howth Golf Course, where a line of white rocks guides you across the fairways. The manicured grass of the golf course comes to an abrupt end as you cross a small peat bog known as the Bog of Frogs. This brings you onto the open shoulder of the Ben of Howth, where you arrive at a path junction. Here you meet the red route, which descends from the masts to the right. A short detour to the right along this trail will bring you to the 171m-high summit of the Ben of Howth, the setting for several romantic moments in James Joyce's *Ulysses*. The hill provides great 360° views, but the foreground is blighted by three communication masts and other associated debris.

Back on the purple route, turn left at the trail junction and descend, passing deciduous woodland, then the local GAA club. You arrive back in civilisation at the end of a suburban street. Follow the markers around a housing estate, keeping generally left at junctions. The route's final section follows a paved pathway through a tunnel of trees – this is the route of the old tramway, which opened in 1901 and was Ireland's last operating tramline before it closed in 1959. The tramway deposits you neatly opposite Howth DART station, back where the circuit began.

Fishing trawlers in Howth Harbour, near the start/finish of the walk.

June 2019
very good.

Fairy Castle Loop

This relatively easy, signed circuit provides a big bang for your buck, with unsurpassed views over Dublin city.

Grade:	2
Time:	1½–2½ hours
Distance:	6km (4 miles)
Ascent:	230m (750ft)
Map:	OSi 1:50,000 sheet 50 covers the route, though the forest trails are marked more accurately on EastWest Mapping 1:30,000 *The Dublin and North Wicklow Mountains*.

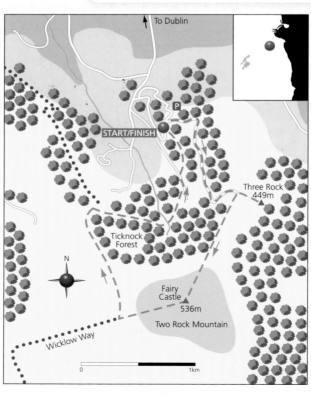

Start & Finish: A trailhead in Ticknock Forest (grid ref: O171240). From the city centre, take the R117 towards Sandyford. Turn right here onto the R113, then take the second turn on the left. This lane climbs steeply to the entrance to Ticknock Forest. Follow the forest drive uphill in a big loop and look out for a track heading off to the right, marked at the bottom by a map board. Park in one of several lay-bys near the start of the track.

Cape Town has Table Mountain, Belfast has Cave Hill, and Dublin has Fairy Castle: all fabulous mountain viewpoints, located right in the suburbs, that provide unsurpassed panoramas of the cities at their feet. Every native or visitor to Dublin should make the journey to the 536m-high summit, to appreciate the bird's-eye view and gain a whole different perspective over the metropolis below.

The walk itself is relatively straightforward, with well-constructed paths and frequent signs in place to aid navigation. In fact, there are numerous signed walking trails in this area, including the Wicklow Way and the Dublin Mountains Way, and the plethora of waymarking symbols is sometimes confusing. For this route, keep following the green footprint icon and you won't go far wrong.

Another slightly confusing feature of the mountain is its name. Most commentators agree that the name of the peak is Two Rock Mountain, an allusion to the double tors that lie on its southeastern flanks. The point marked as Three Rock Mountain is really just a shoulder, again identified by three granite crags. The title Fairy Castle is a reference to the actual cairn that sits atop a large, megalithic tomb at the summit of Two Rock.

The summit tomb is one of several megalithic monuments that can be found dotted around these hills. Today, the granite tors and megalithic sites must vie with some rather more modern accoutrements – a plethora of communication masts. Fortunately these are gathered in one spot on the shoulder of Three Rock, and do not impede the summit views.

Finally, a note of caution: though the paths and signposts mean this route is accessible to a wide range of walkers, you will cross open mountain terrain and the normal rules of hillwalking still apply. Make sure to carry plenty of warm clothing and avoid walking in poor visibility.

The Walk

From the map board, pass around the metal barrier and begin to head uphill along a tarmac road. Climb through one large switchback, then continue on the road through the trees all the way to the base of the massive communication masts that marks the shoulder of Three Rock. The main transmitting station is owned RTÉ, whose signals have been broadcast from here since 1978. Though the masts are an unwelcome urban element, there is no denying the fantastic views north over the city and Dublin Bay.

One of three granite outcrops at the top of Three Rock Mountain.

The tarmac ends here and the road splits into three tracks. The signed loop walk turns right, but it is well worth making a short detour to visit the three rocks that give the shoulder its name. Continue straight ahead at the junction, following the route signed for the Dublin Mountains Way. Just 200m further on, at the top of a rise, you will find the bulbous granite outcrops that form the area's most distinctive natural landmarks. On top of the central tor you will discover four bowl-shaped depressions: these are bullauns, probably used for grinding in Early Christian times.

Return to the junction and turn left to resume the signed loop walk. Follow a gravel, then an earthen trail along the edge of the forest. When the trees end the path continues ahead, climbing over open, heathery mountainside.

At the top of Two Rock is a trig point and the cairn known as the Fairy Castle. The summit markers sit atop a circular structure some 25m wide and 2m high, built of rock but now cloaked in a layer of turf and vegetation. This is a megalithic passage tomb, which has never been opened, though archaeologists believe it contains a central burial chamber. The boardwalk that encircles the summit is

The Fairy Castle Loop is well signed, and passes beside a forest between Three Rock Mountain and Fairy Castle.

The cairn and neolithic passage tomb that mark the 536m summit of Two Rock Mountain.

designed to allow walkers to appreciate the scene while protecting the site from erosion.

The other notable factor of your arrival on top is the sudden expansion of the view. On a clear day, the panorama extends north beyond Dublin as far as the Mourne Mountains. But it is the vista to the south that has suddenly opened up, with many of Wicklow's highest peaks now ranged along the skyline before you. It is a fantastic viewpoint, and a generous reward for the relatively small effort exerted to reach this point.

Turn right at the summit and follow a wide trail that descends gently along the ridge. The wild foreground and mountainous backdrop give the impression that you are now in the heart of the hills. At the next junction turn right again and descend across more open slopes, then along the left side of a forest. This is another spot where city views filling the scene ahead.

At the bottom of the path, turn right onto a gravel track. A short distance later, a marker post signs the route left onto an earthen footpath. Follow this trail as it sweeps left past young pines and descends to a track. Turn right here and follow the track back to the tarmac drive. The map board where you started the route is now just 100m away to the right.

Jan 2019, first walk since moving to Ireland. Greystones - lovely cafes!

Bray Head Coastal Path

This linear cliff path traverses a wild headland and finishes with an ascent to a fantastic coastal viewpoint.

Grade:	2
Time:	3–3½ hours
Distance:	10km (6 miles)
Ascent:	290m (950ft)
Map:	OSi 1:50,000 sheet 56, or EastWest Mapping 1:30,000 *Wicklow East*.

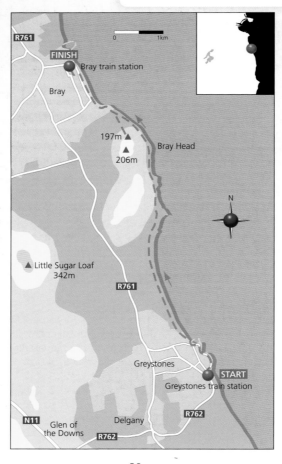

Start & Finish: The route starts at Greystones train station (grid ref: O298122) and finishes at Bray train station (grid ref: O270188). The two stations are located at the southern end of Dublin's DART line, as well as being part of Irish Rail's intercity network. This is a linear walk, and the easiest way to return to your starting point is by rail – there are between one and three trains per hour every day between the two destinations. Both stations have car parks nearby.

Bray Head is to southern Dublin what the Howth peninsula is to the north side of the city: a rugged headland inaccessible by road, but circumnavigated by a popular coastal path that cuts around its steep, seaward slopes. Long views across the Irish Sea give a great sense of space, yet the route is conveniently accessible by train at both ends.

The path was originally built by railway engineers to aid the construction of the train line. After the railway was finished in 1855, the path was retained as a public amenity. Walkers and train passengers continue to enjoy the spectacular coastline, but subsequent rail owners have regretted the decision to route the track this way due to the ongoing costs of maintaining such a wild stretch of line. The track has been realigned six times since opening, and now negotiates four tunnels, the largest of which is 1km long.

The path is well constructed throughout and progress along the coast is scenic yet straightforward. As well as the cliff path, there is also an opportunity to climb to the massive cross that marks a 197m high point on Bray Head. The ground here is steep and rugged, but it is a detour that should not be missed because the headland makes a superlative lookout point across Killiney Bay and the eastern Wicklow Mountains.

By beginning in Greystones and walking the cliff path first, then finishing with ascent of the headland, a wonderful half-day's walking can be had right from the Dublin suburbs. Throw in the comfort of a rewarding snack in one of the interesting cafés around Greystones train station or along Bray's seafront promenade, and you have a really enjoyable day out.

The Walk

With your back to Greystones train station, turn right along the road. Take the first right after 150m, along a lane signed to The Cliff Walk. At the end of the lane, climb across a footbridge that spans the railway tracks. The seafront is now just a short distance ahead and to the right.

Once at the waterfront, turn left and follow the road north along the coast. Pass the marina, then take the first lane on the right in front of a convenience store. Pass in front of Greystones Sailing Club, and shortly beyond this the road dwindles to a gravel footpath.

Descending towards Greystones on the southern side of Bray Head.

Continue ahead between two fences. The path makes a gradual ascent to reach a point about 70m above the sea, then begins to contour around the headland. The airy location provides a great feeling of space, offset by the constant reassurance of a fence on the seaward side. There are glimpses down onto coastal pinnacles and the rocky foreshore below.

There are also several places that allow a view over the railway line and the various tunnels that have been blasted through the rock. The route is furnished with several information boards, and one provides detail on the construction of the line, as well as a tragic accident that occurred in 1867 when a train broke through a wooden viaduct.

The path soon swings left around the northern slopes of the headland. You will notice the Brandy Hole marked on the map here. This is a large sea cave with a back entrance, which was once used to smuggle spirits, tea and silk on night-time missions from France. Continue along the path, and before long you pass the trailside ruins of Lord Meath's Lodge. This gatehouse was used to collect a toll of one penny from people who wanted to walk along the cliff path.

As you approach the town of Bray, the first real piece of urban infrastructure you pass is a car park on the left. If you want to make the highly recommended detour to the top of Bray Head, look for a set of concrete steps leading up from a gap in a stone wall just 20m before the car park. The bottom of the path is also signed with a series of walking waymarks.

Follow the concrete steps up into woodland, with the path soon turning to an earthen trail studded by rocks and tree roots. Side paths branch off in various places but you should continue straight ahead,

View over Bray Head's double railway tunnels. The train line was completed in 1855.

following the most obvious trail and climbing directly up the steep slope. The trees soon begin to dwindle, and the large concrete cross that marks the high point comes into sight ahead. Follow the path to a wonderful viewpoint at the base of the cross, which was erected in 1950 to mark the Holy Year. Here you can savour fantastic views north across Killiney Bay to Howth, and inland towards the eastern Wicklow Mountains.

   To return to the coastal path reverse your ascent route. Now turn left and descend to the end of Bray beach. Follow either the beach or the wide promenade north until you reach the aquarium, around two thirds of the way along the waterfront. Turn left here onto Albert Avenue, and pass under the train tracks. Then take the next right onto a pedestrian walkway known as Albert Walk. Bray train station – and the end of the route – is located at the end of the lane.

Looking north across Killiney Bay from the 197m summit of Bray Head.

Sept 19.
tough section over heather

Prince William's Seat

This short but varied circuit visits three mountain landmarks, with great views across Dublin city and the Wicklow Mountains.

Grade:	3
Time:	3–4 hours
Distance:	10.5km (6½ miles)
Ascent:	400m (1,310ft)
Map:	OSi 1:50,000 sheets 50 and 56, or EastWest Mapping 1:30,000 *The Dublin and North Wicklow Mountains.*

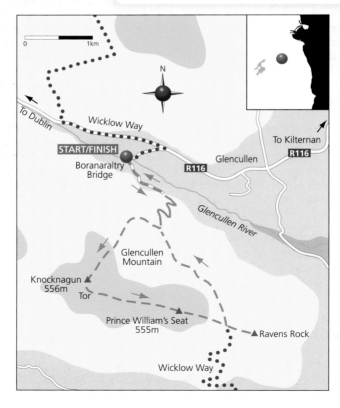

Start & Finish: Boranaraltry Bridge, which crosses the Glencullen River around 2km west of Glencullen village (grid ref: O168206). From Dublin, Glencullen is most easily reached via the R117 Enniskerry road. Turn right in Kilternan and follow the R116 through Glencullen village, then turn left 1.5km later and descend to the river. There is space for about six cars in narrow lay-bys either side of the bridge. No additional parking is available further along.

This short but scenic circuit straddles the border between counties Dublin and Wicklow. As well as marking the political boundary, this ridge of mountains marks a change of landscape. To the north, the views are still dominated by Dublin city. But turn 180° to the south, and the vista is filled by row upon row of interlocking ridges.

It is a neat little circuit that includes an impressive variety of terrain. You pass from fertile valley through thick forest to heathery hillside and summit crags. Route-finding is relatively straightforward – the signposts of the Wicklow Way are followed at the beginning and end of the circuit, and there are paths to guide you across much of the high ground. The only exception is the climb from the edge of Glencullen Forest to the top of Knocknagun. Here you must cross open mountainside, and negotiate rough heather and tussock grass underfoot. The difficulties last little more than a kilometre, however.

Many of the route's main landmarks are the subject of cartographical confusion, with different maps giving the mountains different names and heights. The mountain referred to here as Knocknagun may be spelt Cloghnagun for example, and may have a height of 555m or 557m, depending on which map you use. There is also some mystery surrounding the origin of the name 'Prince William's Seat'. Surveyors from the Ordnance Survey attributed the name to the ridge's easternmost summit, and there may be a link with the 1821 visit of King George IV and Prince William. However, others suggest that the name placement was an error. Part of these uplands were owned by the Fitzwilliam family from the mid 1500s to the late 1600s, and there are literary references to a big rock near Knocknagun where gentlemen used to rest during hunting expeditions. It seems feasible that 'Fitzwilliam's Seat' might refer to Knocknagun's conspicuous granite tor and have nothing to do with British royalty or the eastern summit at all.

The Walk

From Boranaraltry Bridge, follow the lane uphill. After 500m you reach the metal barrier that marks the entrance to Glencullen Forest. Pass through the pedestrian gate and continue ahead along a gravel track. The first part of the track offers beautiful, open views across the fertile valley of

On the track in Glencullen Forest, with the slopes of Knocknagun rising ahead.

Glencullen to Fairy Castle. It is not long, however, before you plunge into a dense pine forest.

Follow the signs for the Wicklow Way though four sharp switchbacks. You then reach a junction where the Wicklow Way continues ahead onto an earthen track, and the main forest road swings right. You will return via the Wicklow Way at the end of the circuit, but for now, turn right and continue to climb along the main track.

The track soon swings left and you get your first views of Knocknagun rising above the trees ahead. Continue on for 300m to the next corner. Where the track starts to turn right across a stream, continue straight ahead and follow a footpath along a firebreak. Within 50m you reach the edge of the forest, with open mountainside ahead.

Your next goal is Knocknagun, the rounded hump that rises ahead and slightly to the right of the point where you emerge from the forest. Begin by continuing straight ahead from the trees, then drop right and cross the stream. You should now make a gradual ascent southwest, crossing heather at first, then tussock grass. Reassure yourself that this is the roughest terrain of the circuit, and conditions will soon improve underfoot. Improving views north towards Dublin reward your effort as you gain height.

There is no cairn at the top of Knocknagun, but if you continue a few metres north of the highest ground you will reach a prominent granite tor, which provides an excellent natural focal point. This is the outcrop used as a resting place for sixteenth-century hunters, which probably deserves the name Fitzwilliam's Seat. The views have now opened up to the south, and there is a fantastic new panorama over the Wicklow Mountains.

The granite tor known as Fitzwilliam's Seat, near the summit of Knocknagun.

The communication mast to the southwest marks the top of Kippure, with Lower Lough Bray clearly visible in the corrie below.

There is also a clear view of Prince William's Seat to the east, with an obvious path making a beeline for the top. Follow the path across a shallow col and all the way to the trig point that marks the summit. Here you are met by a different, coastal vista. The flat metropolis of Ireland's capital sprawls back from Dublin Bay to the north, contrasting with the green, rolling hills of the Wicklow seaboard to the south.

Two paths head east from Prince William's Seat. Take the right-hand trail and descend gradually to a junction with a rough track. This is the Wicklow Way. If you want to visit Raven's Rock, turn right onto the track, then turn left just 15m later at a junction of trails. The path leads easily through the heather for the short distance to the rocks, which is really another small granite tor. The coastal views from here are, if anything, even better than from Prince William's Seat.

When you are ready, return to the Wicklow Way track and turn right. The waymarking posts will now guide you all the way back to the start. Follow the track across a slight rise, then drop back into the upper reaches of Glencullen Forest. Soon you reach the junction you passed near the start of the circuit. Continue straight ahead here, and retrace your initial steps back to Boranaraltry Bridge.

A walker sits on top of Raven's Rock, contemplating the view towards Prince William's Seat.

The Wicklow Way:
An Overview

The 127km-long Wicklow Way was Ireland's first long-distance walking trail, and remains one of the most popular multi-day routes in the country. It forges a path from the southern suburbs of Dublin, across wild moorlands, high mountains and wooded valleys, to finish in the County Carlow village of Clonegal. As well as providing a fantastic journey in its own right, the trail has also been incorporated into the international E8 walking route, which extends across Europe for 4,700km from Cork to Istanbul.

Frequent waymarking posts mean the route is well signed throughout, and there are stiles, footbridges and constructed pathways wherever necessary to aid your progress. The route can be walked in either direction, and the entire Wicklow Way takes around seven days to complete. In this book we highlight the first four days of the trail, covering the northern half of the route from Dublin to the foot of Wicklow's highest mountain in Glenmalure. This is the best part of the longer route; it provides a real sense of journey from metropolis to wilderness, takes you past the most dramatic mountain scenery, and spends the least amount of time along roads.

The four days can either be walked separately or linked together into a multi-day experience. To walk each day on its own you will need to consider the transport arrangements necessary to access a linear route. Fortunately there are bus connections to the start and finish of all stages. To get the most out of the route, it is well worth taking the time to walk the stages back to back. This is worth considering even if you are a local more used to one-day excursions in the hills; the sense of journey and full immersion in the social atmosphere of the trail is only really possible on a longer trip. The route attracts walkers from many countries and you should find that a natural camaraderie builds up as you meet the same people along the path and in the hostels each evening.

If you use your initiative it is also possible to adapt the route, making short detours to visit particular landmarks along the way, or using the long-distance trail as a way of linking other one-day circuits together. See

A Wicklow Walking Odyssey on p. 4 for inspiration regarding some of the options made possible by the trail.

Walkers intending to walk the stages back to back will find a range of overnight accommodation options along the trail. We provide details of the main accommodation providers at the start of each day's description, and you will find a more comprehensive listing (and a host of other information) on the website www.wicklowway.com.

You may also like the idea of a baggage-transfer service, which allows you to walk each day with nothing but a light day-pack. In this case, contact **Wicklow Way Baggage** (Tel: 086 2698659; www.wicklowwaybaggage.com), who will transport a large bag from one stage to another for €7.50.

The four days of the Wicklow Way highlighted in this book encompass roughly half of the 132km-long route, and cover the most interesting and scenic sections of the trail. However, the route continues south from Glenmalure for a further three days, with overnight stops in the villages of Moyne, Shillelagh and Clonegal. Here the high mountains are replaced by rolling hills, and there is a greater reliance on forest tracks and minor roads. If you want to complete the remainder of the route you will need OSi 1:50,000 sheets 61 and 62. Full details of this part of the trail can be found in various publications including Barry Dalby's *The Wicklow Way Map Guide*.

Reflection of Glendalough's round tower, County Wicklow.

Wicklow Way Day 1 – Marlay Park to Knockree

The first day of Ireland's most famous long-distance walk takes you from the Dublin suburbs, over two 500m-peaks, to a remote north Wicklow valley.

Grade:	3
Time:	6–7 hours
Distance:	21km (13 miles)
Ascent:	650m (2,130ft)
Map:	OSi 1:50,000 sheets 50 and 56, or EastWest Mapping 1:30,000 The *Dublin and North Wicklow Mountains*.

Start & Finish: The Wicklow Way starts at the main car park for Marlay Park (grid ref: O155267). This is in Rathfarnham along the R133 Grange Road, c. 9km south of Dublin city centre. *By car:* from the M50, exit at Junction 13. North of the motorway, turn left at a roundabout and follow the R113 to Grange Road. There are two entrances to Marlay Park on the left side of the road – park inside the easternmost entrance, about 2km from the motorway junction. *By bus:* take the No. 16 from Upper O'Connell St in central Dublin; alight at the Marley Grange stop opposite the park entrance.

The day finishes at a parking lay-by on the road just south of Knockree Hill, 200m west of An Óige's Knockree Hostel (grid ref: O190150). *By car:* follow the M11 to Junction 6a, then head west along the R117 to Enniskerry. From here, continue west along the road signed to Glencree. After 2.5km, turn left, then sharp right, and follow signs to the hostel. *By bus:* take the No. 185 from Bray DART station, passing through Enniskerry, all the way to the last stop, which is a forty-minute walk from the hostel.

The Wicklow Way begins in Marlay Park, 300 acres of suburban parkland that includes a Georgian manor house, craft centre, managed woodlands and various recreational facilities. You may want to allow extra time to explore the grounds before you set out onto the route proper. Once you begin walking, it is not long before you leave the city behind and climb into the Dublin Hills. Here you pass through several forestry plantations to reach popular vantage points near the summits of Fairy Castle and Prince William's Seat, landmarks that are described in their own right on p. 16 and p. 24. The trail then crosses into County Wicklow and reaches Knockree at the end of the day, with the big hills looming ahead for Day Two.

The main accommodation providers near Knockree, and the end of Day 1, include **Knockree Youth Hostel** (Tel: 01-276 7981; www.knockree. hostel.com), and **Oaklawn B&B** (Tel: 01-286 0493; www.oaklawnhouse. com), 1km east of the hostel. A range of alternative accommodation can also be found in the nearby village of Enniskerry.

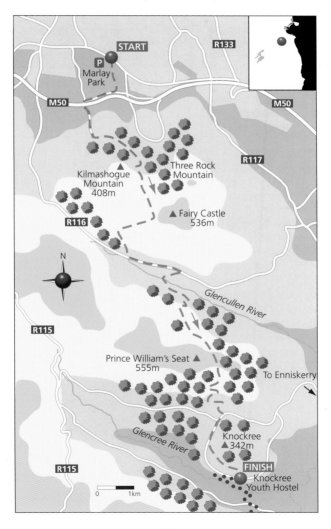

Wicklow Way walkers beside Kilmashogue Forest on the northwestern slopes of Two Rock Mountain.

The Walk

The official start of the Wicklow Way is marked by a plaque at the southern end of Marlay Park's main car park. The route is well signed through the park – it begins beside a grassy playing area, then follows wide paths through a beautiful section of woodland and along the banks of the Little Dargle River.

When you arrive at a T-junction, turn right onto a path that runs parallel to the M50 motorway. Continue across a car park and turn left out of the exit gates. Now turn right and descend along a road to a junction. Turn left here and pass under the M50 motorway, then bear left at a roundabout. This minor road climbs steadily for 1km to reach the entrance to Kilmashogue Forest. This is where you really begin to feel you have swapped an urban environment for nature.

Soon after entering the forest, bear left onto a track. It is a gentle climb around the eastern slopes of Kilmashogue Mountain, with fine views across the city where there are gaps in the trees. Around 2.5km from the forest entrance, turn right onto a rocky path that climbs along the edge of the plantation. Where the trees end, you

The Wicklow Way trail on the southern side of the Glencullen valley.

suddenly find yourself surrounded by open mountain moorland. Continue climbing to a T-junction. Though the signed route turns right here, it is well worth making a quick 500m detour to the left to reach the large cairn known as Fairy Castle, which crowns 536m-high Two Rock Mountain. The summit provides extensive views and hides a megalithic tomb – see p. 18 for full details.

Back on the Wicklow Way, descend steeply to reach a road – the R116 – in the Glencullen valley. Turn left here and follow the tarmac for 1.5km, taking care to avoid passing traffic. Now turn right onto Boranaraltry Lane and descend across the Glencullen River. Climb to the end of the lane, where a gate provides entry to Glencullen Forest.

Continue ahead along a gravel track, climbing through a series of switchbacks. Look out now for a left turn onto an earthen path. This climbs through the forest and emerges onto open moorland near the top of Prince William's Seat. The official route continues ahead along a constructed pathway, but anybody with energy to spare should consider a detour to the 555m-high summit, which will add around 700m to your overall distance. To do this, veer right when you exit the trees and follow a rough path to the summit trig point, which provides another fine 360° panorama. Descend back to the Wicklow Way via another path that heads left (southeast) from the top.

After crossing the summit moorland, the official trail drops south into the trees of Curtlestown Wood. The descent is enlivened by good views over Great Sugar Loaf to the east. Follow the markers through several track junctions to reach the Glencree road. Turn right here, then turn left onto a narrow lane after 200m. Follow the tarmac for 800m, then turn left onto a path that traverses around the hill of Knockree. A final descent brings you to a minor road just west of the youth hostel, and the end of Day 1.

On the shoulder of Prince William's Seat,
heading south along the Wicklow Way.

Wicklow Way Day 2 – Knockree to Roundwood

This day takes you into the high mountains and past some stunning scenery, with an optional detour to the top of a 725m-high peak.

Grade:	3
Time:	6–7 hours
Distance:	21km (13 miles)
Ascent:	690m (2,260ft)
Map:	OSi 1:50,000 sheet 56, EastWest Mapping 1:30,000 *Wicklow East*, or Harvey Superwalker 1:30,000 *Wicklow Mountains*.

Start & Finish: The day starts at a parking lay-by on the road just south of Knockree Hill, around 200m west of An Óige's Knockree Hostel (grid ref: O190150). *By car:* take the M11 to Junction 6a, then head west along the R117 to Enniskerry. From here, continue west along the road signed to Glencree. After 2.5km, turn left, then sharp right, and follow signs to the hostel. *By bus:* take the No. 185 from Bray DART station, passing through Enniskerry and continuing all the way to the last stop. This leaves you a forty-minute walk from the hostel.

The section finishes in the village of Roundwood, which is located along the R755 (grid ref: O190039). **St Kevin's Bus** (Tel: 01 281 8119; www.glendaloughbus.com) runs daily services linking Roundwood to Glendalough, Bray and Dublin.

This route brings you into the heart of the Wicklow Mountains, almost exclusively off-road, along mountain paths and forest tracks. On offer is a lofty view over Ireland's highest waterfall and expansive coastal and mountain vistas. There are several opportunities for detours, most notably to reach the summit of 725m-high Djouce, one of the most popular peaks in the range.

The panorama across Lough Tay from the southern slopes of White Hill is worth noting: 'A great revelation of height and space comes when you look west from this place, for now before you, beyond the huge cleft of Luggala, splendid mountains sharp with crag and abrupt slope rise to the sun ... six thousand acres of loneliness!' These words were written by J. B. Malone, an Irish hillwalking enthusiast who pioneered the country's long-distance walking trails when he proposed and established the

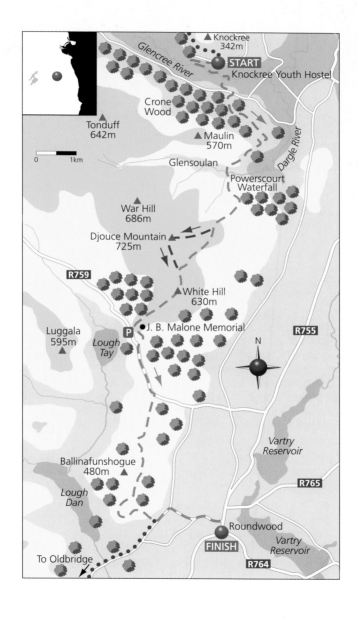

The route crosses boardwalk on the southern shoulder of Djouce Mountain.

Wicklow Way. The Wicklow Way was officially opened in 1982, and Malone died in 1989. There is a memorial to him beside the trail, fittingly placed above the view he held so dear.

When it comes to the end of the stage, most walkers stay either in the hamlet of Oldbridge, or in the larger village of Roundwood. Accommodation options in Oldbridge include the **Wicklow Way Lodge** (Tel: 01 281 8489; www.wicklowwaylodge.com), or, 2km north of the trail on the route to Kanturk Mountain, **Lough Dan House** (Tel: 01 281 7027; www. loughdanhouse.com). Roundwood provides a larger range of services, with numerous accommodation options. The closest place to the Wicklow Way is **The Skylark's Rest** hostel (Tel: 087 091 0342; www.skylarksrest.com). **Tóchar House** (Tel: 01 281 8247; www.glendalough.connect.ie/tocharhouse) and **The Coach House** (Tel: 01 281 8157; www.thecoachhouse.ie) are both centrally located and attached to pubs/restaurants.

Alternatively you may want to camp in the Adirondack shelter located along the trail some 3.5km south of Oldbridge (grid ref: T149991). This basic wooden hut has three sides and a roof, and a raised sleeping platform that can hold up to five people.

The Walk

From the lay-by just south of Knockree Hill, head south onto a forest track. After 500m, turn left onto path that brings you to the grassy bank of the Glencree River. You can now enjoy a delightful stretch of walking, following the river downstream for 1km. Now cross a footbridge and climb along another track to a road. Turn left here and follow the tarmac for 250m to the entrance to Crone Wood.

Turn left through Crone Wood car park, past a map board that indicates the route ahead. Continue along the main forest track for a short distance, then turn left and climb steadily to a clear-felled area with wide-ranging views north and east across Glencree and the Powerscourt Estate. A short distance further on you reach another spectacular view, this time over Powerscourt Waterfall, at 121m, the highest waterfall in Ireland.

Continue ahead, enjoying several more views over the waterfall before you veer right, following a rocky path across a patch of replanted trees. The climb comes to an end when you pass through a gap in a fence and old stone wall. You now arrive at a path junction where the Wicklow Way turns left (the summit of Maulin is a short detour to the right here).

Descend to the banks of the Dargle River, which winds down the base of wild Glensoulan shortly before its plunge over the Powerscourt Waterfall. Cross a footbridge over the river and begin to climb again, now following a wide path along the edge of a forest. Cross a couple of stiles over a stone wall, then climb along a broad moorland trail that rises up the northeastern flank of Djouce. As you gain height, the wide coastal views to the east get better and better.

Before long, you reach the top of the eastern ridge, and another path junction. The official Wicklow Way turns left here, traversing around the mountain's eastern flank. However, to continue to the actual summit, veer right at the junction and climb steadily over the remaining 170 vertical metres to the top. This is a sustained effort, but the reward is to stand at the top of one of the most popular and distinctive peaks in Wicklow. Djouce's 725m-high trig point tops an angular rock outcrop and the views extend far and wide in every direction.

Descend along a wide trail that heads southwest along the summit plateau. After 300m, veer left onto a steep path that brings you down to

On the boardwalk above Lough Tay.

There are periodic map boards along the trail to help you find your way.

another junction, where you rejoin the Wicklow Way. Continue straight ahead onto a length of boardwalk, which guides you south, over the hump of White Hill. Descending from this hill you come to a large boulder with an adjacent plaque. This is the memorial to J. B. Malone, and the accompanying view over Lough Tay and Luggala is quite breathtaking.

Follow a path across a patch of clear-felled forestry, then turn right to reach a car park beside the R759. From here, head left along the road for almost 1.5km, then turn right into another forestry plantation. Follow a series of signed forest tracks for 4km, sometimes walking deep within mature trees and sometimes enjoying more open views across the surrounding countryside. The trail then sweeps around to the left and descends to meet a minor road.

The Wicklow Way turns right onto the road and continues along the tarmac for 2km to the hamlet of Oldbridge. Many walkers detour off the official route here to spend the night in Roundwood. To do this, turn left when you join the road, then turn right 500m later. Continue straight ahead for 1.5km to arrive in the centre of Roundwood.

A memorial plaque commemorating J. B. Malone, the founder of the Wicklow Way.

Wicklow Way Day 3 – Roundwood to Glendalough

The long-distance path traverses low mountain slopes and crosses three wooded valleys on its way to the celebrated vale of Glendalough.

Grade:	3
Time:	3½–4 hours
Distance:	13km (8 miles)
Ascent:	360m (1,180ft)
Map:	OSi 1:50,000 sheet 56, EastWest Mapping 1:30,000 sheets *Wicklow East* and *Lugnaquilla & Glendalough*, or Harvey Superwalker 1:30,000 *Wicklow Mountains*.

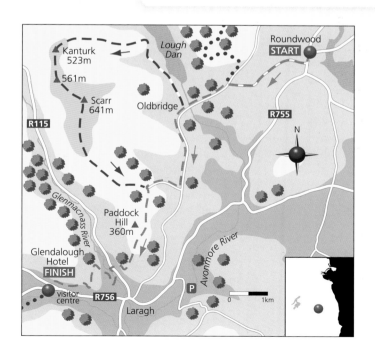

Start & Finish: The route starts in the village of Roundwood, on the R755 (grid ref: O190039). **St Kevin's Bus** (Tel: 01 281 8119; www.glendaloughbus. com) runs daily services linking Roundwood to Glendalough, Bray and Dublin.

The day finishes beside The Glendalough Hotel (grid ref: T124969), on the R757 in Glendalough valley, roughly 3km west of Laragh.

T he third stage of the Wicklow Way is one of the route's shortest sections. After the previous two days you may be glad of the opportunity to move at a more leisurely pace and treat the stage as a partial rest day. Alternatively you may be full of energy, and keen to include a fantastic detour off the recommended route. Either way you will pass more great scenery as you traverse along the lower slopes of Scarr mountain, and will cross three distinct valleys as part of the journey. The day finishes in Glendalough, the most famous and popular valley in Wicklow, where a host of new walking opportunities awaits.

The first 6km of the route from Roundwood follows minor roads, which you might be able to avoid if you can arrange a lift from a friendly accommodation provider. The optional detour involves adding the circuit over Scarr and Kanturk, a route that is described in full on p. 89. This mountain circuit is highly recommended but not waymarked, so you will need to have full navigational skills to complete it. The ideal way to add the circuit to your itinerary is to spend the previous night at Lough Dan House, Oldbridge, rather than descending to Roundwood. If you can do this, the detour will add an extra 8km and 370m ascent to your day.

Once you arrive in Glendalough there are plenty of opportunities for extra exploration. The sixth-century monastic city, for which Glendalough is so famous, lies through an archway 100m west of Glendalough Hotel. Around 150m east of the hotel, Glendalough Visitor Centre explains the history of the valley in more detail. There are also some fine, one-day walking routes that explore the cliffs and mountains around the Glendalough. The Spinc Loop (p. 105) and Camaderry Circuit (p. 100) are both great options, and start and finish within a kilometre of Glendalough Hotel.

In terms of accommodation, there are two main options within the valley itself. An Óige's **Glendalough International Hostel** (Tel: 0404 45342; www.anoige.ie) is a popular choice, while **The Glendalough Hotel** (Tel: 0404 45135; www.glendaloughhotel.com) also has a restaurant and bar. A range of alternative accommodation can also be found in the nearby village of Laragh.

The Walk

Unless you can arrange a lift, the first 6km of your day involves walking along minor roads. Turn west in the centre of Roundwood, following the road signed to Lough Dan. Take the first left, then veer right at a fork to reach a T-Junction. This is where you rejoin the Wicklow Way. Turn left here, then descend across a bridge over the Avonmore River to reach a junction in the hamlet of Oldbridge. If you want to add the circuit over Scarr and Kanturk, turn right here and refer to p. 89.

To remain on the official Wicklow Way, continue straight ahead at the junction in Oldbridge, and follow the road for another 2.5km, climbing then

Signposts keep you on the right track near Oldbridge.

descending to cross another small stream. Around 400m beyond the stream, turn right onto a vehicle track. At the end of the track cross a stile, which brings you out onto open terrain beneath the southern shoulder of Scarr mountain (this is where you rejoin the route if you have added the

The route crosses a footbridge over the beautiful Glendasan River.

circuit over Scarr and Kanturk).

Turn left at the corner of a forestry plantation and follow a path that climbs south alongside the trees. This brings you to a stretch of track across Paddock Hill, where you can enjoy far-reaching coastal views to the east. The vista changes again as you pass over the brow of the hill, with the angular summit of Lugnaquilla and the cliff-lined corrie of Glendalough both now visible to the south.

A swift descent brings you to the R115. Follow the road left for 200m, then turn right through replanted woodland. Cross a footbridge over the Glenmacnass River then, on the opposite bank, turn right at a fork in the path. Climb through more mixed woodland to reach a forest road, where you should turn right again. You are now walking beneath the dark pines of Brockagh Forest.

Continue straight ahead at a track junction, then climb out into the open. Near the top of the rise, turn left. As the trail sweeps round to the right and begins to descend, you are greeted by a spectacular view over Glendalough, the Upper and Lower Lakes tightly enclosed within the deep surrounding basin.

Pass through a gate and re-enter the forest, then turn left and descend through a series of switchbacks. You will need to negotiate four tightly-placed stiles to reach the R756. Cross straight over this road and continue downhill to arrive in Glendalough opposite the Glendalough Hotel. The youth hostel is located 300m along the road to the right.

The view along the Glendalough valley from the eastern base of Brockagh Mountain.

Wicklow Way Day 4 – Glendalough to Glenmalure

Follow the path over a 550m-high ridge to arrive in remote Glendalough, near the base of Wicklow's highest peak.

Grade:	3
Time:	4–5 hours
Distance:	14km (9 miles)
Ascent:	450m (1,480ft)
Map:	OSi 1:50,000 sheet 56, EastWest Mapping 1:30,000 *Lugnaquilla & Glendalough*, or Harvey Superwalker 1:30,000 *Wicklow Mountains*.

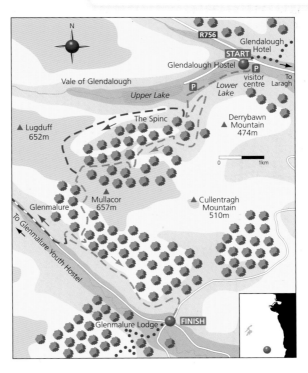

Start & Finish: The route starts beside The Glendalough Hotel (grid ref: T124969), on the R757 in Glendalough valley, roughly 3km west of Laragh. **St Kevin's Bus** (Tel: 01 281 8119; www.glendaloughbus.com) runs daily services linking Glendalough to Roundwood, Bray and Dublin. The day finishes beside The Glenmalure Lodge, at the crossroads in Glenmalure valley (grid ref: T107908). **Wicklow Way Bus** (Tel: 0404 29000; www.wicklowwaybus.com) runs daily services from Glenmalure to Laragh, and on to Rathdrum train station which connects with rail services to Dublin.

The fourth day of the Wicklow Way provides a fitting finale to the longer route. It climbs out of Glendalough and passes over a lofty mountain ridge before descending into Glenmalure, thus linking two of Wicklow's most famous valleys. The entire route is on footpaths and forest tracks.

The first landmarks you pass are Glendalough Visitor Centre and the sixth-century monastic city, both of which provide worthy reasons to pause your journey. Once you begin the ascent itself, there are two route options. The official route climbs south along a series of forest tracks. However, if you have never walked along the Spinc, the high cliffs that border the southern edge of Upper Lake, it is worth considering a more scenic alternative here. By following the national park's signed Red Route instead of the Wicklow Way, you will arrive at the same place on top of the ridge, but will be able to include the thrilling sensation of surveying Glendalough from atop these lofty cliffs.

The finish in Glenmalure leaves you perfectly placed to round your journey off with an ascent of Lugnaquilla, the highest mountain in Leinster. The trip up this peak is one of Ireland's classic walks, see p. 125. If you intend to climb this mountain, the best option is to detour off the Wicklow Way during the descent and stay in An Óige's rustic **Glenmalure Youth Hostel** (Tel: 01 830 4555; www.anoige.ie), at the head of the valley. It has no electricity or running water, and is open daily June to August and on Saturday nights only at other times.

Another rustic option is the Adirondack shelter located along the trail around 2km north of Glenmalure (grid ref: T092924). This basic wooden shelter has three sides and a roof, and a raised sleeping platform that sleeps up to five people. Or, if you prefer more comfort, near the crossroads at the end of the stage are **The Glenmalure Lodge** (Tel: 0404 46188; www.glenmalurelodge.ie) – meals are served all day – or **Coolalingo B&B** (Tel: 0404 46583; www.coolalingobandb.com).

The Walk

From the front of The Glendalough Hotel, head east along the road for 150m and turn right towards Glendalough Visitor Centre (the centre provides a fascinating insight into the history and natural history of the valley). Cross the car park to reach a footbridge in its southwestern corner. Here there is a map board illustrating various routes, including the Wicklow Way.

Cross the footbridge and turn right along a wide path known as the 'Green Road', which is likely to be busy with tourists. After 200m a footbridge on the right provides access to the monastic city founded by St Kevin in the sixth century. The site includes a range of Early Christian buildings and crosses, and is well worth a visit.

Following the signs through Lugduff Forest, at the start of the climb out of Glendalough.

Follow the Green Road for 1.5km, passing through mature oak woodland on the bank of Lower Lake. Continue straight ahead until you reach the park information office (a small white cottage). If you want to visit the shore of Upper Lake, make a quick out-and-back detour 100m to the right here.

Around 20m beyond the park office, the Wicklow Way turns left up a path signed for Pollanass Waterfall. Climb a series of steps, with the falls tumbling down a narrow rock gorge beside you. At the top of the path turn left onto a forest track, which soon brings you to a track junction.

This is where you must decide if you want to climb the mountain via the official Wicklow Way or via the park's Red Route. To include a more scenic trip along the cliffs of the Spinc, turn right at this junction and follow the route signed by the red arrows. These markers will lead you along the cliffs before veering left and arriving at the col between Lugduff and Mullacor. See the Mullacor Circuit on p. 109 for a full description.

The official Wicklow Way brings you to the same col, but climbs the forested slopes of Derrybawn Mountain instead. To remain on this route, turn left at the junction above Pollanass Waterfall. Cross two bridges and follow the track northeast for about 600m, then sweep around a sharp right-hand bend and climb steadily south through the trees. Follow the waymarkers through several clearly marked junctions before emerging onto high, open moorland at the col between Lugduff and Mullacor.

Signposts and boardwalk mark the trail in the col between Lugduff and Mullacor.

In clear conditions this col provides a fantastic vantage point. To the southwest the massive bulk of Lugnaquilla sprawls above Glenmalure. To the north the Camaderry ridge is backed by Tonelagee, the third highest summit in the region. It is worth pausing to savour these views fully.

Cross the col on a length of wooden boardwalk, heading south towards another forestry plantation. Turn left along the top of the trees, then turn right and descend a series of rock steps. This brings you to a forest track, where you should turn left.

If you have decided to stay at Glenmalure Youth Hostel, the best option is to leave the official route partway through the descent. Continue along the signed tracks for roughly 1.5km until you reach an oblique junction where the signed route veers left. Keep right here and descend steeply to the road that runs along the base of the valley (the path is clearly marked on the EastWest Mapping sheet). Turn right onto the tarmac and continue for 2km, past the end of the road and over a ford, to reach the hostel itself.

Trail-side sign showing the way ahead.

To descend along the official route, follow the signs through several track junctions as you make your way gradually down through the forest. Eventually the trail swings northeast and you drop down to meet a road beside a bridge. Turn right here for the final 400m before finishing at the crossroads beside The Glenmalure Lodge.

Seefingan Circuit

A compact circuit close to Dublin, visiting four easy summits and one of the finest prehistoric monuments in the region.

Grade:	4
Time:	3½–4 hours
Distance:	10km (6 miles)
Ascent:	560m (1,840ft)
Map:	OSi 1:50,000 sheet 56, EastWest Mapping 1:30,000 *Lugnaquilla & Glendalough*, or Harvey Superwalker 1:30,000 *Wicklow Mountains*.

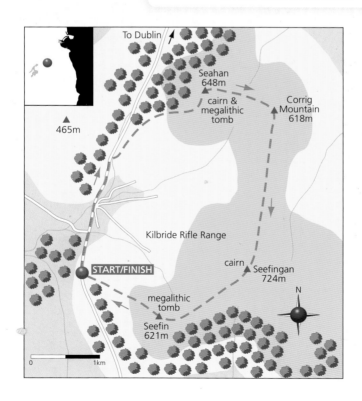

47

Start & Finish: A small lay-by at the southwestern corner of Kilbride Rifle Range (grid ref: O063169). Exit the M50 at Junction 11, and follow the N81 towards Blessington. Turn east off the N81 in Brittas, then follow your map to the start. There is space to park three vehicles at the initial lay-by, and a few parking places further north along the road.

Now for a hill-walk with a difference: a mountain route where the mountains play second fiddle to another feature of the landscape. While the four hills visited here form a compact, scenic circuit, it is what sits on top of them that makes the route remarkable. Scattered around their summits lie no fewer than five Neolithic tombs. In fact, the area has been likened to an Irish Valley of the Kings, with its unusual density of ancient burial sites, many encased within elaborate stone cairns, constructed up to 5,000 years ago.

Of the five tombs on the circuit, one is a wedge tomb and the others are all passage tombs. The most impressive is atop Seefin and was excavated in the early 1930s. As you approach the site, you see a huge stone cairn, 24m in diameter and 3m in height, with a surrounding kerb of boulders. Circle to the north to find the exposed entranceway, shored up by a lintel and posts of solid rock decorated with faint etchings. Beyond this, a narrow passage stretches inward for 7m; if you are slim enough you may be able to squeeze along it, or you may peer through the collapsed roof of the central burial chamber. The inner chamber has five alcoves, which would once have held human remains and other artefacts. It is an immensely evocative spot.

This is also a good hill-walk in its own right. It is easily reached from Dublin city and includes a visit to the top of Seefingan, the second highest point in County Dublin at 724m. The outing is essentially a journey around the edge of the Kilbride Rifle Range. On days of scheduled firing, red flags fly on top of the poles at the entrance to the military camp in the centre of the circuit. The route keeps to the edge of the range, however, so even on these days you can complete the walk as long as you are careful to keep outside the signs that mark the range boundary.

Though there is a clear path underfoot for much of the circuit, these are rounded hills with little to define them topographically, and you should take care with navigation in poor visibility. There is also some boggy terrain to cross – particularly in the col between Corrig and Seefingan – so the route is best avoided after periods of wet weather. Note too that the various maps suggest different names and heights for some of the peaks, and the route's first mountain may either be marked as Seahan or Seechon.

The start of the mountain path to Seahan, which passes between Seahan Forest and Kilbride Rifle Range.

The Walk

From the lay-by, begin by heading north along the road. Descend straight across a dip at Shankhill Crossroad, then climb past Kilbride Military Camp. Continue to follow the tarmac until you come to the edge of Seahan Forest on your right. Turn off the road to the right just before this plantation, dropping into a broad ditch and crossing Seechon Brook. Cross a simple stile over a fence, then pick up the remains of an old track. Turn left here and climb gently northeast, passing between the edge of the forest and the northern boundary of the firing range.

At first the track is boggy in places, but as you gain height it becomes firmer underfoot. The gradient increases as you swing east and climb to the corner of the plantation. Here the track turns into a broad, peaty path, and veers northeast to reach the top of Seahan (648m).

There are three megalithic tombs scattered around this summit, though they are all now partly ruined or covered by vegetation. The eroded trig pillar sits atop one sprawling cairn, which measures 24m wide by 2m high and has never been opened. A short distance to the east lies a passage tomb some 21m in diameter, with the flat capstone that covers the central chamber exposed and clearly visible. Finally, a short distance west of the summit, you should be able to spot a cluster of boulders that are actually the shattered remains of a wedge tomb.

Now turn east and follow an obvious path that descends across a shallow col, then climbs to 618m-high Corrig. This is the only mountain on the circuit without a Neolithic monument. Turn south at the top, still

The path between Seahan and Corrig Mountain.

following a well-worn path as you make your way towards the broad dome of Seefingan. The col that separates the two peaks can be very wet in places and progress is often awkward. The path largely disappears amongst the bog, but re-emerges as you begin the climb up the northern shoulder of Seefingan.

The actual summit of Seefingan (724m) is marked only by a warning sign for the firing range. However, it is a superb viewpoint for the peaks of western Wicklow, with landmarks including Mullaghcleevaun and the Blessington Lakes to the south and southwest, and the prominent communication mast at the top of Kippure to the east. From here, head west for a couple of hundred metres to the edge of the summit dome. Here you will find the mountain's most notable feature, a Neolithic cairn that probably covers a collapsed passage tomb, and is crowned by a trig pillar.

From the cairn, follow a clear path that descends southwest to the boggy col beneath Seefin. Note, however, that this path crosses the boundary into the military range, so you should avoid it if firing is taking place. Instead, head south from the tomb for 300m before turning southwest to reach the southern side of the same col.

Either way, it is a short climb from the col to the Neolithic tomb that crowns the summit of Seefin (621m). This is one of the most impressive prehistoric sites in Wicklow, so take some time to explore the site properly.

Descend from Seefin in a westerly direction, following a steep, peaty path towards the corner of Kippure Forest. Here you can duck under some wire and join a good path that descends between the trees and the boundary of the firing range. The path deposits you neatly back at the road and lay-by where your vehicle should be waiting.

The collapsed roof allows you to see into the central chamber of the neolithic passage tomb that lies at the summit of Seefin.

Kippure and the Two Lough Brays

Two stunning lakes, a climb up a steep crag and the highest summit in County Dublin – what more could you want from a 7km route?

Grade:	4
Time:	2½–3½ hours
Distance:	7.5km (5 miles)
Ascent:	350m (1,150ft)
Map:	OSi 1:50,000 sheet 56, EastWest Mapping 1:30,000 *The Dublin and North Wicklow Mountains*, or Harvey Superwalker 1:30,000 *Wicklow Mountains*.

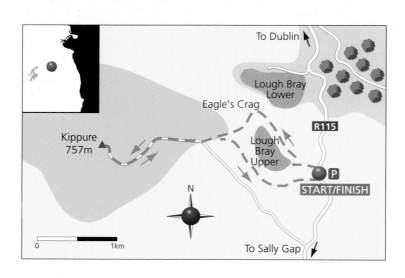

Start & Finish: A gravel lay-by in an old quarry above Lough Bray Upper (grid ref: O143153), on the R115 Military Road, some 4.5km north of the Sally Gap. There is parking for about ten cars.

Cutting into the eastern slopes of Kippure, Lough Bray Upper and Lough Bray Lower form two of the most impressive high-altitude lakes in Wicklow. This route circumnavigates the upper lough, beginning at its shore, then climbing the steep prow known as Eagle's Crag to reach the corrie rim above. As well as offering fantastic views over the lakes, the trip includes the top of 757m-high Kippure, which lies on the county border and is treasured by summit-baggers for its title as highest point in County Dublin.

During the last Ice Age, Kippure lay near the head of a glacier that flowed eastwards and created the Glencree valley. As the main ice sheets retreated, small high-altitude glaciers continued to chisel out deep corries on the flanks of the mountain. The surrounding accumulations of moraine debris would eventually act as dams, collecting the meltwater in deep pools and creating the twin loughs we know today.

Eagle's Crag is another reminder of the past, its name recalling the white-tailed eagle, for which species a nesting site was recorded on the cliffs above the lakes until the 1830s. Unfortunately, by the end of the nineteenth century human persecution had led to the species' extinction in Ireland, and today peregrine falcons or kestrels are the main birds of prey to be glimpsed soaring on the cliff-side thermals.

The walk itself follows a clear path around the upper lough and up Eagle's Crag. The climb up the crag is steep, and though it is only 100m high, it will be most enjoyed by confident walkers. Many people choose to circumnavigate the lake on its own, without adding the side-trip to the summit of Kippure. If you do decide to visit Kippure, there is the option of either crossing open ground, or following a traffic-free access road. The summit experience is somewhat compromised by the existence of a massive communication mast, but the wider views are expansive.

Given the proximity of steep cliffs, it goes almost without saying that you should avoid walking along the rim of the corrie in poor visibility.

The Walk

The path starts opposite the lower end of the parking area. From here, follow an obvious earthen trail that descends steeply from the road. Cross a stream at the base of the slope, then continue ahead to a path junction beneath the upper lough. If you want to visit the shore of the lake, keep left here and make the 200m detour to the water's edge.

Return to the junction and this time turn sharply left. Climb to the top of a low, heather-covered ridge that runs along the eastern side of the lake.

Approaching Eagle's Crag, between Upper and Lower Lough Bray.

The peaty path is easy to follow, and takes you past several large boulders. Towards the end of the ridge, descend slightly, now enjoying a view over the lower lough to the large, private house on its opposite shore.

Between the two lakes, a rocky prow – Eagle's Crag – dominates the scene. You should be able to make out the path that climbs steeply up its southern side. The trail consists of eroded peat and rock, and you will need to use your hands in several places. Though the ground is unrelentingly steep, the prow is just 100m high, and it is not long before you reach the top. Here a lofty outcrop provides a wonderful vantage point, with the two lakes spread out on either side below.

View over Lough Bray Upper from the top of Eagle's Crag.

Now follow the path that curves south around the rim of the upper lough. This peaty trail passes through heather and bilberries and offers more fabulous views over the water below. If you want to visit Kippure, leave the path after roughly 400m and strike off across open ground to the west. Soon the massive communication mast that marks the summit comes into view. It may not be pretty, but it provides an unmistakable navigational marker. A short while later the access road also becomes visible below and to the left of the mast.

You must now decide whether you want to take the purist's way to the top – avoiding the road – or else use the tarmac to help you. As the ground underfoot is rather wet initially and then covered by rough heather, most people take the easy route along the road. Head southwest slightly and aim to join the lane at a small concrete bridge with an adjacent shelter. Turn right here and follow the road uphill, possibly returning to open ground to shortcut the dog-leg near the top.

Mist swirling around the communication mast that marks the 757m summit of Kippure.

The summit itself is one of the least attractive in the region, thanks to the 110m-high mast, various buildings and an assortment of communications paraphernalia. It is the oldest television transmitter site in the Republic of Ireland (RTÉ began transmissions here in 1961). The trig point is located beside the mast and the views over the surrounding peaks are extensive, so try to concentrate on those instead.

From the summit, retrace your steps to the concrete road bridge, then head left and return to open ground. The distinctive cone of Great Sugar Loaf now provides an obvious landmark on the horizon. Aim slightly to the left of this as you descend and you will soon find yourself back at the rim of Lough Bray Upper. Continue to drop through the heather and bilberries for 20m to rejoin the rim path. Turn right here and resume your previous journey around the lake.

The path soon sweeps east and begins to descend along the ridge at the southern end of the lake. The trail becomes fractured here as it negotiates several marshy patches, but if you keep sweeping east around the corrie you will soon pick it up again. Descend across a stream, then climb the opposite bank to rejoin the Military Road. Turn left along the tarmac to reach the parking area 100m later.

Maulin Circuit

Jan 19
good pull up.

March 2020
start of Covid
lockdown.

A compact and popular mountain circuit that follows paths and waymarks for much of the distance.

Grade:	3
Time:	2½–3½ hours
Distance:	7km (4½ miles)
Ascent:	420m (1,380ft)
Map:	OSi 1:50,000 sheet 56, EastWest Mapping 1:30,000 *The Dublin & North Wicklow Mountains*, or Harvey Superwalker 1:30,000 *Wicklow Mountains*.

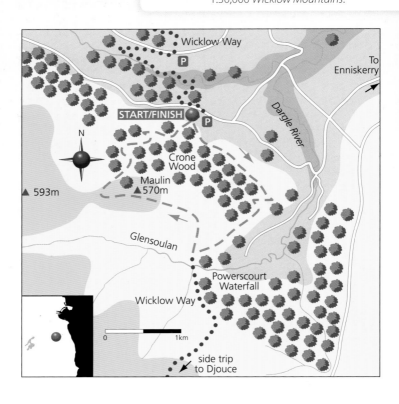

Start & Finish: Crone Wood car park (grid ref: O193142). From Enniskerry, drive south along the R760 for 3.5km, then turn right. Follow this minor road across the Dargle River, then veer northwest to reach the parking area. The car park is locked at 8 p.m. during summer months and earlier in winter.

The ascent of 570m-high Maulin is one of the most popular mountain walks in Wicklow, and rightly so, because it is an accessible and straightforward circuit that offers all the reward of climbing a wild summit, but with relatively little effort or risk. It is almost as close as you can get in Ireland to a 'recreational' mountain, with established paths and tracks to follow throughout. It is even partly waymarked because the route follows either the Wicklow Way or a national looped walk for much of the distance.

However, it is still very much a mountain, and there is steep ground to avoid on the northern summit slopes. It is essential to be properly prepared because, at almost 600m in height, the exposed summit is prone to rapidly changing weather. It is a compact peak, so the walk fits easily into an afternoon. But do leave time to savour the views from the summit, especially to the north and east across Great Sugar Loaf and Dublin Bay. There are also fantastic views from the rim of the Dargle valley across to Powerscourt Waterfall.

Walkers who are looking for a longer outing can consider adding a side trip to the summit of 725m-high Djouce Mountain. Including this out-and-back detour doubles the day's distance and total ascent, and merits a difficulty grade of 4. Alternatively you could combine the route with a one-hour side trip to the base of Powerscourt Waterfall. See p. 60 for details of that route.

The Walk

Before you set out it is worth consulting the map board at the top of the car park, which indicates the route of both the Wicklow Way and the national looped walk, and allows you to get your bearings. Begin by following a forestry track uphill for a short distance to a junction. Keep left here, following signs for the Wicklow Way. The track climbs steadily to a clear-felled area with wide-ranging views north and east across Glencree and the Powerscourt Estate. After about forty-five minutes you come to a spectacular view of Powerscourt Waterfall, which, at 121m, is the highest waterfall in Ireland.

Shortly after this viewpoint you come to a map board for the national looped walk. The looped walk turns right here, but this route continues ahead along the main track, still following signs for the Wicklow Way. There are several more views of Powerscourt Waterfall before you veer right,

At the start of the forest trail in Crone Woods.

following a rocky path across a patch of replanted trees. The end of the climb comes when you pass through a gap in a fence and old stone wall.

Just beyond the wall you arrive at a junction where the Wicklow Way turns left, dropping conspicuously into Glensoulan then climbing the eastern shoulder of Djouce Mountain. If you want to include a side trip to Djouce, head out and back along this path. To continue along the Maulin circuit, turn right at the junction. Follow a good, rocky path due north along a broad shoulder that is thick with heather. There is an old boundary wall to the right, and fine views of Great Sugar Loaf beyond. Less than 500m later the path swings abruptly northwest, the gradient eases, and there is under a kilometre of easy walking to the small cairn that marks the summit of Maulin.

From the summit, avoid the temptation to descend directly north into Crone Wood because the slopes here are very steep. Instead continue west along an obvious, informal path, heading towards the col beneath Tonduff South. There is an old stone boundary wall on the right and you should follow this as it trends north. Descend a steep section where the trail is quite rough, then pass through a gap in the wall to reach a much better path. This swings back northeast to reach a wooden gate and stile at the edge of Crone Wood. Cross the stile and join a forestry track, where you meet the red waymarks of the national looped walk.

The Wicklow countryside as seen from the slopes of Maulin.

The descent through the forest to the car park is marked throughout by red waymarks, though the signposting is not always obvious. Look out in particular for waymarks nailed to tree trunks. The route drops steeply though the thick plantation, following a series of switchbacks with occasional views over the Glencree valley below. Towards the bottom of the slope you turn right onto a track, which leads back to the parking area where the route began.

View towards Great Sugar Loaf from Maulin's summit cairn.

Powerscourt Waterfall from Crone

Follow a series of woodland paths on a backdoor approach to the base of Ireland's highest waterfall.

Grade:	2
Time:	2–2½ hours
Distance:	6.5km (4 miles)
Ascent:	260m (850ft)
Map:	OSi 1:50,000 sheet 56, EastWest Mapping 1:30,000 The Dublin & North Wicklow Mountains, or Harvey Superwalker 1:30,000 Wicklow Mountains.

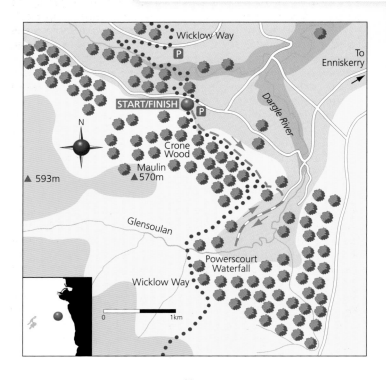

Start & Finish: Crone Wood car park (grid ref: O193142). From Enniskerry, drive south along the R760 for 3.5km, then turn right. Follow this minor road across the Dargle River, then veer northwest to reach the parking area. The car park is locked at 8 p.m. during summer months and earlier in winter.

P owerscourt Waterfall is one of Ireland's iconic natural attractions, set in the foothills of the Wicklow Mountains on the southern edge of the Powerscourt Estate. It is formed by the nascent Dargle River, where it flows over a series of high slabs and cliffs at the head of a glacially carved valley. At 121m it claims to be Ireland's highest waterfall, though the allegation remains a point of debate. At any rate it is a very impressive cascade, pouring down in several beautiful braids into the thickly wooded glen below. It is particularly impressive after heavy rain, when it becomes a thundering torrent likely to drench anyone approaching within 50m of the base.

The waterfall and surrounding valley are privately owned by Powerscourt Estate, who have opened the site to the public. The vast majority of visitors to the waterfall arrive by car or by walking along the access road. However, there is also a little-known alternative approach, almost secretive in its nature. It is not a formal walking route, but requires you to link several sections of old track that lead into the densely wooded Dargle valley from the adjacent forestry area at Crone Wood. In fact this route begins in the same place as the Maulin Circuit (see p. 56), and can be easily combined with an ascent of that mountain if you prefer a longer outing.

The Powerscourt Estate is open daily, with the exception of two weeks around Christmas. Opening times are 10.30 a.m. to 4 p.m. in winter, and 9.30 a.m. to 7 p.m. in summer. There is a charge for entering the grounds by car, but no charge for walkers entering on the route described.

The Walk

Leave Crone Wood parking area and follow a forestry track uphill for a short distance to a junction. Keep left here, following signs for the Wicklow Way. The track climbs steadily to a clear-felled area with wide-ranging views north and east across Glencree and the Powerscourt Estate. You then pass through a long tunnel of beech trees, before emerging into a broad clearing.

Just beyond the clearing, look out for a smaller track that veers off to the left. Descend along this for a short distance to reach a gate. Beyond the gate, the track becomes heavily overgrown with gorse and bracken. Avoid the obstruction by turning right and joining an informal path that descends steeply through the pine trees.

The path that descends through Crone Woods towards Powerscourt Estate.

Powerscourt Waterfall is the highest waterfall in Ireland at 121m high.

You soon arrive at an old benched track, which descends gently along the upper edge of a beautiful beech forest. Turn left and follow this track downhill for a few hundred metres, where it also becomes overgrown. Again you should bypass the blockage by turning right and following a faint, informal path down a steep grassy slope into the beech woodland.

After a short descent through the trees you emerge onto the surfaced access road for Powerscourt Waterfall. Make a careful note of where you join the road as you will need to find this point again on the return journey. Now turn right and follow the road gently uphill. Look out for sika deer, red squirrels and the Giant Redwoods that were planted in the estate more than 200 years ago. After just five to ten minutes you arrive at the base of the waterfall. Facilities include public toilets and a small café, which is open every day during the summer and weekends only at other times of the year.

Retrace your outward journey to return to the car park at Crone Wood. To add a view of Powerscourt Waterfall from high above the Dargle valley, turn left along the Wicklow Way when you reach the main forestry track. Roughly 500m later you arrive at an outlook with a fine, elevated view across the woodland canopy to the waterfall. From here either retrace your steps back to the start, or continue along the route of the Maulin Circuit (see p. 56 for further details of that route).

ROUTE 13:
Great Sugar Loaf

This iconic little peak features a short but steep ascent that is guaranteed to raise a smile from the whole family.

Map: OSi 1:50,000 sheet 56, or EastWest Mapping 1:30,000 *Wicklow East*.

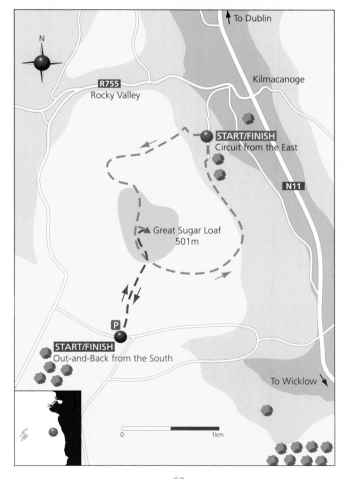

Despite its modest height of 501m, Great Sugar Loaf is one of Wicklow's most recognisable peaks. Its conical profile lends it a distinctly volcanic character, and it stands in sharp contrast to the more rolling contours of many of the other Wicklow mountains. Standing slightly aloof from the rest of the range, this natural landmark provides a familiar focal point from countless surrounding locations.

This is not a difficult peak to climb. The rocky slopes are challenging enough to give a real sense of fulfilment, yet the climb is so short it offers a perfect afternoon out for families and casual walkers.

The mountain derives its name from its resemblance to the conical sugar cakes that were popular during the nineteenth century. It owes its distinctive shape to its peculiar geology. While most of the surrounding hills are made of Devonian granite, Great Sugar Loaf is composed of Cambrian quartzite, an erosion-resistant rock. It was completely covered during the last Ice Age, but as the glaciers melted, its summit was exposed while the retreating ice sheets scoured its flanks to give us the pointed, craggy summit we know today.

Given the mountain's popularity, I make no apology for describing two routes to the summit. The first is a straightforward, out-and-back trip that can be completed in little over an hour. This is the most popular way to climb the peak, and it can be very busy on a sunny weekend. The alternative circuit is longer, less frequented and more satisfying, and could be described as the connoisseur's route to the top.

Paths are followed throughout both routes, though the longer circuit negotiates a myriad of trails that is sometimes confusing. It is not unusual to see children as young as three attempting the mountain, and there is no doubt it offers a perfect introduction to mountaineering for energetic, well-supervised children. Be warned, however, that the final ascent crosses very steep rock and necessitates hands-on scrambling over loose stones. If you are contemplating bringing young children here, it would be wise to complete the ascent unaccompanied first to assess the level of difficulty for yourself.

The wide path that leads up the southern slopes of Great Sugar Loaf.

Out-and-Back from the South

Grade: 3
Time: 1–1¼ hours
Distance: 3km (2 miles)
Ascent: 210m (690ft)

Start & Finish: A car park at the southern base of Great Sugar Loaf (grid ref: O235119). Take the N11 from Dublin towards Wicklow and turn off at Junction 9, which is signed for Glenview. On the western side of the N11, turn left up Red Lane. The steep, narrow road climbs to the top of the shoulder beside Great Sugar Loaf. Park on the right in a car park marked by a stone entrance arch.

The Walk

From the car park, walk around the metal gate and begin to follow a wide earthen trail towards the mountain. Climb gradually to a rock-studded area just beneath the main slopes. The path then forges uphill, over the rocks, to reach a flat area partway up the mountain's western flank.

Continue to a junction of paths, then turn right. You are now on the final ascent to the summit, and the slope is very steep. You will need to use your hands as you scramble over the rocks, and care is needed to avoid slipping on loose stones underfoot. The trail broadens here to allow several possible ascent routes. Choose between an eroded gully or the slopes nearby, and if a particular rock step is too high for you, you will generally find an easier route by stepping to one side.

The slope only relents as you arrive at the summit itself. There is no cairn to mark the high point, but the compact top provides plenty of natural drama. Rocky outcrops underfoot combine with fantastic 360° views over Dublin city, the central Wicklow Mountains and a long stretch of coastline. On a clear day you may even be lucky enough to see the peaks of Snowdonia across the Irish Sea.

Descend by reversing your outward route, taking care not to dislodge rocks onto walkers approaching from below.

Circuit from the East

Grade:	3
Time:	2–2½ hours
Distance:	5km (3 miles)
Ascent:	380m (1,250ft)

Start & Finish: In front of Kilmacanoge GAA pitch (grid ref: O244141). From Dublin, turn off the N11 at Junction 8, signed to Roundwood and Glendalough. Cross to the western side of the N11, then, just before a roundabout, turn left onto Quill Road. Just 30m later, turn right up a narrow lane signed to Fitzsimmons Park GAA Grounds. Continue almost to the end of the lane, where you will find the sports ground on the right. Park in a lay-by outside the club gates, where there is space for at least eight vehicles.

The Walk

From the parking area, join a footpath that runs along the right-hand side of the GAA grounds. This brings you to open scrubland beneath Great Sugar Loaf. Keep right at the first fork and continue along the path, then take the third turn on the left, opposite a mound of boulders. Follow this trail uphill, climbing initially through gorse and scrub, then up a steep, grassy slope.

This brings you to a heather-clad col on the northern shoulder of the mountain. Turn left here, then left again to join a wide trail that runs along the ridge. There are now fine views east over the Wicklow Mountains, with Djouce particularly prominent on the skyline.

Keep left at the next junction and climb gradually around the eastern side of a hummock. The conical shape of the summit now fills the scene ahead. Veer right at the next fork and follow a rocky path up to a flat area just west of the summit. Here you join the main path described above; turn left and scramble up the steep rock slopes to the summit.

After appreciating the summit views, return to the flat area and turn left to resume the circuit. Descend south along a rocky path until the angle of descent eases, then continue ahead for another 100m to reach a point just above a wide patch of short grass. Look carefully here to locate a faint grassy footpath that turns left off the main trail.

Follow this footpath east, with the trail consolidating underfoot as you descend. You are now heading towards the wooded valley of the Glen of the Downs. Around 400m above a farm building, turn left onto a clearer, earthen path that swings left above a quarry.

At the base of the slope, keep right in front of a thicket of gorse, then turn left and right at the following two junctions. You are now back on a clear footpath that passes around the eastern base of the mountain. Descend to a copse of beautiful deciduous woodland, keeping right at a fork shortly after you enter the trees. It is not long now before the path arrives at the end of a tarmac road. Follow the road ahead, and you will find yourself back at the GAA grounds just a few hundred metres later.

The path on the northern shoulder of Great Sugar Loaf.

July 2020 — would not do again as a circular. Too much burden

ROUTE 14:

Djouce and War Hill

This circuit combines one of Wicklow's most popular summits with a trip through a wild and lonely valley.	**Grade:**	4
	Time:	4½–5½ hours
	Distance:	14km (9 miles)
	Ascent:	660m (2,170ft)
	Map:	OSi 1:50,000 sheet 56, EastWest Mapping 1:30,000 *The Dublin and North Wicklow Mountains* or *Wicklow East*, or Harvey Superwalker 1:30,000 *Wicklow Mountains*.

Start & Finish: A parking area above Lough Tay along the R759 (grid ref: O169075). Access the area either via the Millitary Road and the Sally Gap, or via the R755 Kilmacanoge–Roundwood road. The car park is marked by a map board for the Wicklow Way, and there is space for at least twelve vehicles. There are several other lay-bys nearby along the road.

The focal point of this route is the summit of the popular, 725m-high Djouce. Though this peak could be visited in a short out-and-back trip in its own right, the addition of a circuit around the northwestern side of the mountain allows a visit to lonely Glensoulan, the summit of War Hill, and the landmark of the Coffin Stone. As well as covering varied terrain, this is an immensely scenic circuit. There are wide-ranging views over the Wicklow mountains and coastline and the early panorama across Lough Tay is quite rightly one of the most celebrated sights in the region.

Though there are no visible remains today, on the upper slopes of Djouce is the site where a French Army Junkers aeroplane crashed on 12 August 1946, with five crew members and twenty-one girl guides on board. Stormy weather had forced the plane off-course, but it landed like a glider on the boggy ground and the main fuselage remained intact. Despite some injuries, all on board survived.

The route follows the Wicklow Way for around half its distance, benefiting from the signposts, paths and boardwalk of the longer trail. There is also an informal path to ease your progress between the summit of War Hill and Djouce. However, the section from Glensoulan to the top of War Hill crosses wild and rough terrain that can be thick with heather,

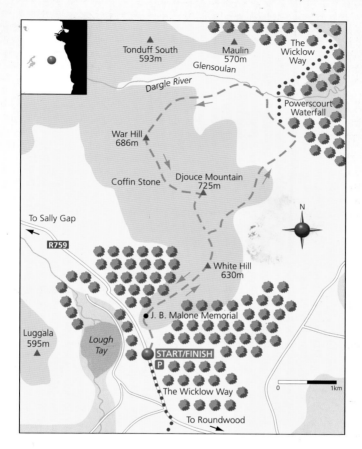

and you will need to rely on your own route-finding skills here. The route presents no particular navigational difficulties, though it is worth waiting for clear conditions to make the most of the views.

The Walk

Begin by heading past the map board at the top of the parking area and joining a vehicle track. Just 50m along the track, turn left onto an earthen path that weaves through a patch of clear-felled forestry. This brings you to the start of a boardwalk, which climbs onto the southwestern shoulder of White Hill. Before long you reach a large boulder with an adjacent plaque commemorating J. B. Malone, pioneer of the Wicklow Way. It is a fantastic viewpoint, and the sight of Lough Tay nestling beneath the towering cliffs of Luggala is surely one of the region's most impressive scenes.

The upper Dargle River cuts through the heart of wild Glensoulan.

Continue to follow the boardwalk over the hump of White Hill, where the views expand to include the Irish Sea to the east. Ahead, the summits of Djouce and War Hill can now also be seen. Descend slightly and cross a stile in the col between White Hill and Djouce. Now climb again, still following the wooden walkway as it makes a steady ascent along the shoulder towards Djouce. Soon you arrive at a junction, where an informal path continues ahead and the boardwalk of the Wicklow Way turns sharply right. Turn right here – you will return along the path ahead at the end of the circuit.

The boardwalk soon comes to an end, and you descend along Djouce's eastern slopes on a narrow footpath. The distinctive, volcanic shape of Great Sugar Loaf lies directly ahead as you contour across to the mountain's northeastern shoulder. At the shoulder, veer right and descend along a broad path to reach a stone wall. Cross the wall, still following the signposts for the Wicklow Way, and descend to a second stile. This is where you leave the waymarked trail and strike out across open country.

The Wicklow Way turns right immediately after the stile, but you should continue straight on, heading towards the foundations of several old stone buildings that can be seen across a stream below. These ruins, along with their attendant lazy beds, are evocative reminders of a previous age.

Follow a faint, grassy path towards the stream, which you cross with the help of a makeshift bridge. Now veer right, past the stone foundations, and descend around the northern base of Djouce. Join the bank of the nascent Dargle River and turn left to head upstream. You are now in the heart of Glensoulan, and the landscape feels pleasantly wild after the well-trodden trail of the Wicklow Way. If you are ready for a break, the riverbank makes an atmospheric place for a rest.

There is no path to guide you, and progress is sometimes awkward between here and the summit of War Hill. Follow the Dargle upstream and cross the tributary that drains the valley between War Hill and Djouce. Shortly beyond this, leave the river and begin to climb the northeastern shoulder of War Hill. The heather is very thick in places, and will continue for most of the way to the top. The rounded summit itself is marked by a tiny cairn and far-reaching views, with the mast to the northwest indicating the top of Kippure.

Turn southeast at the summit and follow a faint path that makes a gradual descent to the col below. You will have to negotiate a few peat hags here, before climbing to the huge boulders that make up the Coffin Stone. This is either a suggestively placed glacial erratic or, as some believe, a megalithic portal tomb, its massive capstone now partially collapsed and the remains of a courtyard visible at the front.

Continue to climb southeast from the stone, following a path to the trig point at the top of Djouce, which is set rather jauntily atop a rock outcrop. The mountain's name comes from the Irish *Dioghais*, which means 'fortified height', and is either a reference to its crowning crag, or to an old cairn that once stood just north of the summit. The views extend far and wide, and it is worth savouring the moment.

Begin the descent by following a wide trail southwest along the summit plateau. After 300m, veer left and descend a steep path that passes the site of the 1946 aeroplane crash. This brings you to the junction with the boardwalk that you passed on your outward journey. Continue straight ahead onto the planks, and retrace you initial steps along the Wicklow Way to the finish.

Is it a megalithic portal tomb? The Coffin Stone, between War Hill and Djouce.

Walker at the 725m summit of Djouce.

Mullaghcleevaun from the North

Visit the shore of Cleevaun Lough then tackle Mullaghcleevaun's steep north ridge on this scenic circuit above Pollaphuca Reservoir.

Grade:	4
Time:	4–5 hours
Distance:	12km (7½ miles)
Ascent:	630m (2,070ft)
Map:	OSi 1:50,000 sheet 56, EastWest Mapping 1:30,000 *Lugnaquilla & Glendalough*, or Harvey Superwalker 1:30,000 *Wicklow Mountains*.

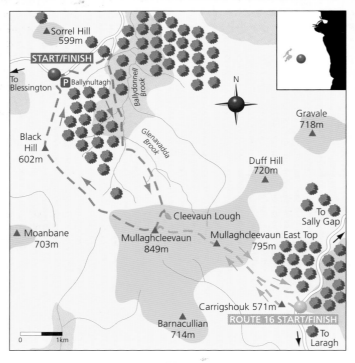

Start & Finish: A car park on Ballynultagh Gap, in the col between Black Hill and Sorrel Hill (grid ref: O044108). Follow the N81 to Blessington. In the centre of the village, take a minor road northeast for 1km, then cross Blessington Bridge. Turn right and follow this road south to the village of Lackan. Fork left here and follow a narrow, bumpy road to Ballynultagh Gap. The car park on the southern side of the road has space for at least fifteen vehicles.

At 849m, Mullaghcleevaun is the second highest summit in Wicklow and the twentieth highest mountain in Ireland. Besides its fine summit views, the peak's most distinctive feature is the steep corrie that cuts into its northern slopes and which has given the mountain its name; the Irish *Mullach Cliabháin* translates as 'summit of the basket', and is almost certainly a reference to its most notable natural feature. The basin is filled by Cleevaun Lough, which, at 686m high, is the highest natural lake in Wicklow.

This route takes you to the shore of the lake, then climbs Mullaghcleevaun's steep north ridge to the summit itself. The descent over Black Hill provides an unsurpassed vista over Pollaphuca Reservoir, or the Blessington Lakes as they are commonly known. This reservoir was created in the late 1930s when the River Liffey was dammed, with the dual purpose of supplying drinking water to the Dublin region and allowing the construction of Ireland's second hydroelectric power station. The water eventually flooded some 5,000 acres of land, making it the largest reservoir in Ireland. Today the shoreline is 56km long, and the entire reservoir is designated as a Special Protection Area in recognition of its importance for the international Greylag goose population.

The first 3.5km of the route follows tracks through Ballylow Forest. These tracks provide easy access into the expanse of moorland that lies to the north of the Mullaghcleevaun massif. Once you leave the forest, you must rely on your own route-finding skills. There is a narrow path on the northwestern shoulder of Mullaghcleevaun, and a track on the final descent from Black Hill, but you will be crossing wild, open terrain for much of the route.

The EastWest Mapping sheet is the best option here, and clearly marks all the tracks you need. (The OSi map does not show many of the forest tracks near the start.) For an alternate route up Mullaghcleevaun from the south, see p. 76.

The Walk

From the car park, head east along the road for 400m. Turn right here and head into Ballylow Forest, following a narrow path along a firebreak. This brings you to a gravel track, where you turn left. After 500m, take the first right turn, following a grassy track that descends through the trees to a junction near an old cottage.

Turn right here and pass through a metal gate. Keep right again at the next junction to reach the edge of the plantation. Now turn left, pass around a barrier, and begin to follow the track south along the edge of the trees. Continue for roughly 2km, sometimes passing through the trees, and sometimes enjoying more open views across the moor to the southeast. At one point the track has been washed away by a stream and you will have to scramble down and up the banks to continue onward.

Keep straight ahead till you come to a large, rusted gate in a clearing on the left. This is where you leave the forest and strike out over open ground. The cone of Mullaghcleevaun provides an obvious target ahead. Cross the stream and climb the slope on the opposite side, picking a line that keeps about 300m to the right of a stream gully. For the next 2km you must negotiate the roughest terrain of the circuit, crossing a mixture of heather, bracken and moorland grass.

The view north from Mullaghcleevaun, showing Ballylow Forest and the expanse of moorland you must cross to reach the mountain.

Cleevaun Lough remains hidden from sight until you are almost on top of it, but keep climbing southeast towards the base of Mullaghcleevaun's northern ridge. You will cross several hummocks before mounting a rise and suddenly discovering the lake filling a hollow at your feet. The lough is backed by steep cliffs and the impressive location combines with shoreline boulders to make this a perfect spot for a break. You will need to gather your energy for the steep ascent of 150 vertical metres that now lies ahead.

When you are ready, leave the lake and begin to climb the ridge that leads up from its western tip. The ground is studded with rocks and steepest at the apex of the shoulder, but an easier gradient can be found by veering a few metres away to the right. The ascent is sustained all the way to the top, but the effort is relieved by superb aerial views over the lake towards Duff Hill.

As you reach the summit plateau, you will need to veer southwest slightly to reach the cairn and trig point. The southern skyline, previously obscured from view, is now revealed ahead, with Tonelagee to the south.

Begin the descent by heading northwest, towards the views over Pollaphuca Reservoir. As you drop off the plateau you should pick up a path which leads easily down Mullaghcleevaun's northwest shoulder. In poor visibility, this path should keep you from heading too far west towards the shoulder of Moanbane.

As the ground evens out at the base of the slope, the path becomes lost amid a maze of peat hags. Continue ahead in a northwesterly direction, soon emerging from the obstacles and descending across moorland grass to reach the col beneath Black Hill. A final, easy climb brings you to the top of this 602m-high hill, whose rounded summit is marked by a wooden boundary post for Wicklow Mountains National Park. A short detour to the west lets you enjoy the best views over the reservoir below.

From Black Hill, descend north to join the end of a stone track. This carries you easily down the mountain's northern slopes and deposits you neatly back at the car park where the route began.

On the northern slopes of Mullaghcleevaun, looking across Cleevaun Lough towards Duff Hill.

Mullaghcleevaun from the South

A short but rewarding route up the second highest summit in Wicklow, with fine views over the lough on its northern side.

Grade:	4
Time:	3–3½ hours
Distance:	8.5km (5½ miles)
Ascent:	570m (1,870ft)
Map:	OSi 1:50,000 sheet 56, EastWest Mapping 1:30,000 *Wicklow Mountains West*, or Harvey Superwalker 1:30,000 *Wicklow Mountains*.

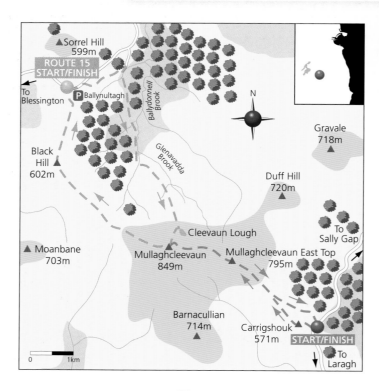

Start & Finish: The end of a track just northeast of Carrigshouk (grid ref: O103053). Approach the area via the Military Road between Sally Gap and Laragh. There is parking space for around four vehicles at the end of the track, and several other lay-bys nearby if you need more room.

This is the easiest and most direct route to the top of Mullaghcleevaun, the second highest peak in the Wicklow Mountains at 849m. It is an out-and-back trip, and includes a visit to the summits of Carrigshouk (571m) and Mullaghcleevaun East (795m). In terms of scenery, the final 2km before the summit are the best. Here you pass along the edge of the steep corrie that cuts into the mountain's northern slopes, providing a lofty vantage point from which to admire Cleevaun Lough below.

In clear conditions the views from the summit of Mullaghcleevaun extend as far as Wales, and the route presents few navigational difficulties. In poor visibility you should exercise caution near the corrie rim, and will probably need to take a compass bearing to ensure the correct line of descent. A faint path is visible in places, but elsewhere you cross untracked ground and must rely on your own route-finding skills.

This is just one of several approaches for Mullaghcleevaun. Other itineraries include a trip from the Sally Gap, over Gravale and Duff Hill, though this option crosses rather a lot of rounded bogland. Alternatively you can approach the mountain from the north – see p. 72 for a full description of this route.

If you prefer a longer outing, this route can also can be combined with Tonelagee (see p. 85). Begin as described here, then head south from Mullaghcleevaun, over Barnacullian and Stoney Top, and descend as described for Tonelagee. This gives a long circuit of 17km, though you should beware of wet and arduous ground along the ridge between Barnacullian and Stoney Top. There are extensive peat hags in this area, which are sometimes so deep they are more like fissures or crevasses in the bog. If you opt for this variation, keep to the eastern side of the ridge to avoid the worst of the obstacles.

The Walk

The sharp hummock of Carrigshouk is an obvious landmark from the Military Road, and features short but steep slabs on its eastern side. In good visibility the rocks can all be clearly seen from below, and it makes an interesting start to the walk to pick a route up through the outcrops to the top.

From the end of the track, walk a few metres south along the road. Leave the tarmac at the hill's northeastern base and begin to pick your way up between the rocks. One good option follows a faint path through a small gully on the hill's northeastern corner, though less steep and rocky

Looking towards Mullaghcleevaun from the summit of Mullaghcleevaun East.

ground can be found on the northern slopes. The mountain's name comes from the Irish *Carraig Seabhac*, meaning 'Rock of the Hawk or Falcon', and you may see some of these birds as you climb.

From the small summit cairn there are already good views over Lough Dan to the east and Tonelagee's corrie to the southwest. To the northwest the rounded, peaty ridge leading to Mullaghcleevaun East is also clearly visible. Descend northwest over heather-clad slopes to reach the col beneath this mountain, then begin the gradual ascent to the top. The ground is rough at first but becomes easier as you gain height, and you should pick up a faint path as you progress.

The summit of Mullaghcleevaun East is marked by a small cairn and several interesting boulder formations. Mullaghcleevaun itself can now be seen to the west. Before embarking on the next leg of the journey, however, you should study the terrain in the col beneath you. Several swathes of exposed peat spread across the saddle, and the easiest passage is to avoid these as much as possible. With some judicious forward planning, and by keeping to the northern side of the col, you should be able to select an easy route.

From the col, begin to climb the grassy slope ahead. Keep to the right and climb around the rim of the corrie to enjoy the best views across the lough below. This is a great piece of walking and it is hard to tear yourself away from the drama of the corrie, but to reach the official summit you must head southeast for a short distance, where you will find the mountain's trig point. Continue a few metres away from the summit and circle the edge of the small plateau to fully appreciate the fantastic views. Pollaphuca Reservoir lies below to the west, Lugnaquilla can be seen to the south, Kippure is marked by its summit mast to the northeast, while the Wicklow coast completes the scene to the east.

The return route is essentially a reversal of your outward journey. As you leave Mullaghcleevaun summit, you may notice a plaque on a boulder commemorating three Wicklow hikers who drowned off Clogher Head in 1945. Later, as you descend from Mullaghcleevaun East, it may be useful to note that you should begin by heading towards Lough Dan. By doing this, you should pick up the path that will ease your progress down the shoulder.

Unless you want to revisit Carrigshouk, you can vary your return by following a narrow path that drops off the northern side of the col beneath the hill. This trail descends gradually around the northern base of Carrigshouk. It then joins a rutted track for a short distance, before dropping left to join a better gravel track. Follow the track back to the road, where your vehicle should be waiting.

A trig point and fine views mark the 849m summit of Mullaghcleevaun.

Luggala and Knocknacloghoge

A spectacular route over neighbouring summits, above the two most iconic lakes in the Wicklow Mountains.

Grade:	5
Time:	4½–5½ hours
Distance:	12km (7½ miles)
Ascent:	780m (2,560ft)
Map:	OSi 1:50,000 sheet 56, EastWest Mapping 1:30,000 *Wicklow Mountains West* or *Wicklow East*, or Harvey Superwalker 1:30,000 *Wicklow Mountains*.

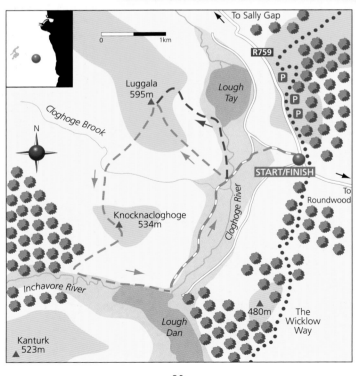

Start & Finish: The gateway known as the 'Pier Gates', located along the R759 above Lough Tay (grid ref: O173065). Access the area either via the Military Road and the Sally Gap, or via the R755 Kilmacanoge–Roundwood road. The black metal gates are set in a stone wall, with an adjacent access sign for walkers. Park beside a track entrance opposite the gates. If you need more space, there are several other lay-bys nearby.

Exploring two mountain summits between Lough Tay and Lough Dan is surely one of the most scenic walks in the Wicklow Mountains. The peaks are wild and rugged, and are connected at their base by a strikingly beautiful valley with the most photographed lakes in the region.

The glen was moulded by the glaciers of the last Ice Age, and Loughs Tay and Dan are classic examples of ribbon lakes – where a series of lakes has formed at the bottom of a U-shaped valley after the ice has melted. Today the valley forms part of the 6,000-acre Luggala demesne, privately owned by members of the Guinness family. The estate has been used as the location for several well-known films over the years. The main building, Luggala Lodge, is located at the northern end of Lough Tay and dates back to 1787.

The remains of lazy beds can be seen in various parts of the valley and deer, common lizards and peregrine falcons are often seen.

We offer two options for reaching the summit of Luggala. One is a straightforward ascent along the southeast shoulder; the other is a steep, challenging scramble up a gully in the middle of the mountain's eastern cliffs, which is only for the experienced, confident walker.

Though the circuit involves no great navigational difficulties, the middle section crosses rough terrain with no path, and precipitous drops mean you should avoid the route in poor visibility. In late summer, swathes of bracken will complicate the descent from Knocknacloghoge, while crossing Cloghoge Brook will be awkward after rain.

The Walk

Pass through the pedestrian gate beside the Pier Gates and walk downhill along the road. Either follow the road all the way to the valley floor, or look out for a wooden pole in a section of fence on the left. This marks a steep footpath that will shortcut the dog-leg in the road.

As you near the valley floor, the road arrives at another gateway. Cross a stone stile beside the gate, then continue straight ahead at the next junction. The road now dwindles to a gravel track, and arrives at a bridge across the Cloghoge River. Cross the bridge, then quickly turn right and climb a large wooden stile. This is where the normal and adventurous routes divide.

Bridge over the Cloghoge River in Luggala Valley at the start of the route.

Normal Route

The vast majority of walkers take this ascent route. From the wooden stile, pass through a metal gate, then continue straight up a grassy path that can be seen climbing the slope in front of you. The path climbs steadily up Luggala's southeastern shoulder, with the grassy terrain turning to peat as you gain height. Follow the path all the way to the summit, where you converge with the adventurous option.

Adventurous Route

From the wooden stile, pass through a metal gate and turn immediately right. Follow the Cloghoge River upstream to the shore of Lough Tay, where the steep eastern cliffs of Luggala tower above the lake.

Take a moment to pick out the route ahead. In the centre of the cliffs, a prominent cone of grass and scree climbs halfway up the slope. Above this to the right, a massive crag juts out from the top of the corrie, with vegetated gullies on either side. The route climbs to the top of the grassy cone, then heads up the gully to the left of the crag. The terrain is not too steep at first, but you will need to use your hands as you gain height; a slip here could have nasty consequences. There are several faint trails over the middle section, which consolidate into a more obvious path as you climb past the left side of the crag. Pause on a secure perch somewhere near the top to take in the wonderful views.

The view over Lough Tay from the adventurous route, which climbs a gully through the centre of the Luggala cliffs.

As you emerge over the lip of the corrie, you reach flatter, heathery terrain. Turn left here and follow a path around the rim and up to the summit. Here you rejoin the 'normal' route described above.

The summit of Luggala is something of an anticlimax, without even a cairn to mark the high point. Descend now in a southwesterly direction. The wetter the conditions, the further west you should go, to ease your crossing of the Cloghoge Brook. Thick heather makes the descent rather awkward, and once you have crossed the river, the initial part of the climb south up Knocknacloghoge crosses rough ground too.

From the north, Knocknacloghoge appears unremarkable, with uniform slopes covered by heather and tussock grass. It is only as you reach the summit that you discover it is strewn with granite outcrops. The southern side of the mountain features numerous exposed boulders and cliffs: unsurprisingly, the Irish name translates as 'hill of the stony land'.

Knocknacloghoge summit is marked by a small cairn and provides a fine 360° panorama. Join a path that heads south and descend past a couple of outcrops. When the trail veers southeast you should leave it, however, and head southwest instead. The slopes here are rough and covered with bracken rather than heather.

As you descend, aim for the forestry plantation on the northern bank of the Inchavore River. Do not head directly for Lough Dan, as steep crags along the southern base of the mountain will bar your progress. Pick your way between the boulders to reach the river, which can be seen in the valley below.

Once in the valley, turn left and follow the riverbank upstream. You will have to negotiate several marshy patches before reaching the spit of white sand at the northwestern tip of Lough Dan. Unfortunately the beach lies on the opposite side of the deep river, out of reach.

Continue ahead onto a well-trodden path that runs along the northern shore of Lough Dan. The path, which is surrounded by thick gorse, exits near a deserted, two-storey house at the northeastern corner of the lake. (If you want a break, it is well worth making a short detour here. Turn right beside the house and follow a smaller path for 300m to reach a secluded beach.)

Back at the deserted house, turn northeast onto a grassy track. This leads along the river and past fields, with native woodland on the opposite bank. You will need to pass through a couple of gates and cross a bridge before arriving at the bridge encountered earlier in the day. Now simply retrace your initial steps – unfortunately uphill this time – to return to the start point.

Beside Lough Dan, at the southern base of Knocknacloghoge.

ROUTE 18:
Tonelagee

This compact route climbs around – or through – a dramatic corrie to reach the third highest summit in Dublin and Wicklow.

Grade:	4
Time:	3–4 hours
Distance:	8km (5 miles)
Ascent:	490m (1,610ft)
Map:	OSi 1:50,000 sheet 56, EastWest Mapping 1:30,000 *Wicklow Mountains West*, or Harvey Superwalker 1:30,000 *Wicklow Mountains*.

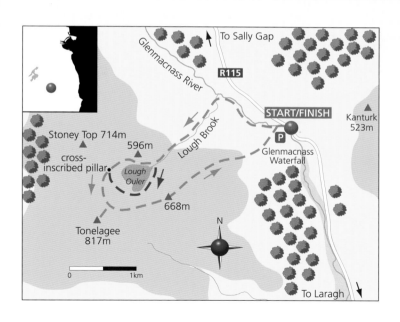

Start & Finish: A large car park above Glenmacnass Waterfall (grid ref: O113030), beside the R115 Military Road, around 7km northwest of Laragh and 10km south of the Sally Gap.

Tonelagee is the third highest peak in Dublin and Wicklow. From most angles its slopes are uniform and not particularly interesting. But approach the summit from the northeast, and you will discover a deep corrie that cuts into its flanks, at the base of which lies heart-shaped Lough Ouler.

Tonelagee translates from Irish as 'backside to the wind', which makes sense when you consider that Ireland's prevailing winds come from the southwest. Both the corrie and lake are classic features of a post-glacial landscape. Indeed, the entire valley, including the 80m-high Glenmacnass Waterfall, owes its form to the scouring movement of past ice sheets.

The route is fairly straightforward from a navigational point of view. You follow informal paths for roughly half the distance, and cross open mountainside for the rest. We describe two options for climbing between Lough Ouler and the summit of Tonelagee: a normal route and an adventurous alternative. The adventurous line follows a series of steep ramps directly up the 200m-high headwall, and is not for the faint-hearted. Most walkers prefer the normal route. Glenmacnass car park can be particularly busy on weekends and during the holiday season. Note that the corrie rim is dangerous in poor visibility, and you may not be able to ford the Glenmacnass River after heavy rain (as there are no alternative crossing places, you will have to chose a different objective if this is the case).

For a longer variation, this route can also can be combined with an ascent of Mullaghcleevaun, see Route 16 (p. 76) for details of the 17km alternative.

The Walk

From the car park, walk upstream along the bank of the Glenmacnass River for roughly 80m. Here a jumble of river boulders provide perfect natural stepping stones. Cross the river here, then turn right along the opposite bank.

Follow the river for another kilometre until you reach the confluence with the outlet stream that flows down from Lough Ouler. Cross this side-stream, then turn left and begin to follow its northern bank southwest. There is a narrow path here to ease your progress through the heather.

After almost 2km you mount a rise and see the lake ahead, backed by steep corrie walls. Continue to the lakeshore, where our two routes diverge.

On the bank of the Glenmacnass River, at the start of the circuit.

Normal Route

When you arrive at Lough Ouler, keep on the lake's northern shore. Follow a narrow path along the shore and up to the shallow col just west of point 596m. From here, follow a path that makes a curving ascent around the northeastern rim of the corrie, climbing steadily all the time.

Shortly before the top you will pass a small standing stone. Made of an upright slab of mica schist, the stone has a roughly carved Latin cross incised on each face. Archaeologists believe it is simply an ancient boundary marker. Continue to climb around the rim, then veer southwest to reach the trig pillar that marks the summit itself.

Adventurous Route

Cross Lough Ouler's outlet stream and pass around the southern shore of the lake. At the lough's southwestern corner you will see a series of grassy ramps climbing diagonally to the right up the back of the corrie. This is your route to the top.

There are few signs of passing feet to guide you, so you must keep alert and rely on your own skills to find the best route. The angle of ascent is relatively benign near the bottom of the slope, but becomes steeper as you gain height, and in the last quarter of the climb you will need to use the grass and heather for support. The easiest terrain can be found by starting up the left-hand ramp, then gradually traversing right, and finishing at the top of the right-hand ramp. You emerge onto the summit ridge roughly 20m north of the cross-inscribed pillar.

The unusual heart shape of Lough Ouler is worth a photo!

Turn left here and follow the rim of the corrie south, then head southwest to reach Tonelagee summit.

Regardless of how you reached the top, the summit views are fantastic. The mountains to the west stand out, where the summit reservoir of Turlough Hill is backed by the mighty bulk of Lugnaquilla, whose massive summit cairn is just visible on the skyline. To the north, the rounded, peaty saddle of the Barnacullian ridge stretches away towards Mullaghcleevaun, providing another, longer access route to Tonelagee.

For the descent, head southeast from the trig pillar. A faint path shows the way. Now sweep east along the ridge, keeping close to the rim of the corrie for more fantastic views over the heart-shaped lough below. Descend across a shallow col and climb slightly to point 668m, still following a visible path.

Now head northwest along a broad ridge. The natural tendency here is to veer further south than necessary, so take care to keep on the correct line. The path dissipates somewhat underfoot, but continue ahead through the grass and heather, then drop down to meet the Glenmacnass River. Cross the river on the same stepping stones you used before, then complete the final 80m downstream to the car park.

Scarr and Kanturk

This memorable route traverses a pair of mid-height peaks, with fine views over Lough Dan and the central Wicklow Mountains.

Grade:	4
Time:	4–5 hours
Distance:	14km (8½ miles)
Ascent:	540m (1,770ft)
Map:	OSi 1:50,000 sheet 56, EastWest Mapping 1:30,000 *Wicklow Mountains West*, or Harvey Superwalker 1:30,000 *Wicklow Mountains*.

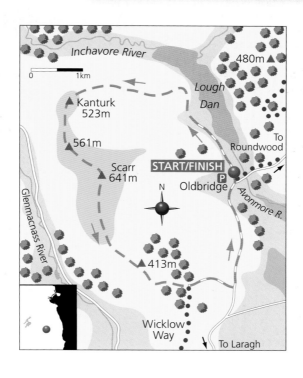

Start & Finish: A lay-by in Oldbridge (grid ref: O 158 019). Oldbridge can be reached from Laragh or Roundwood. From Roundwood, turn west, following signs to Lough Dan. In the hamlet of Oldbridge, turn right, still following the Lough Dan signs. Park 250m later in a gravel lay-by on the left, located just before a junction with a minor road, where there is space for around ten vehicles.

A cursory glance at the map would not engender much excitement about climbing 523m Kanturk or 641m Scarr. The two mid-height summits seem to lack high corries, sharp ridges, or anything else to define their slopes. But this is a route that most walkers find more enjoyable and memorable than they had thought possible.

The route begins with a scenic treat, traversing high above the shore of Lough Dan. The summits themselves boast a surprising amount of character, with Kanturk distinguished by a maze of rock outcrops and Scarr by its narrow summit ridge. And the massif's location right in the heart of the Wicklow Mountains ensures incredible views throughout.

Lough Dan is the largest natural lake in County Wicklow, and one of the most scenic. It is part of the glacial ribbon-lake system that also includes Lough Tay to the north. Access to the shore is limited by the private ownership of the surrounding land, but the route includes fine views along its 2.5km length.

The route follows well-defined paths across all the high ground, making navigation relatively simple. There are sections of road walking at the start and finish of the circuit, with a total of almost 4km along the tarmac. These lanes see little traffic, however. If you prefer a shorter route, it is also possible to descend directly to Oldbridge from the summit of Scarr. Follow a path along the mountain's northeastern shoulder, then descend southeast to reach a forestry plantation. Head along a firebreak to a clearing, where you join a track. Follow this as it veers right to reach a lane, then turn left to return to the junction where you started the route.

The Walk

From the parking lay-by, begin by heading northwest along the road. Climb steadily along the tarmac, passing first through mixed forest, then past more open, pastoral countryside with fine views over Lough Dan. After 1.5km the road crosses a bridge and turns sharply left. Around 60m beyond the bridge, a narrow wooden gate on the right marks the start of a footpath. A walking sign and access notice confirm that this is the official route to Kanturk.

Follow the path through a fenced copse of woodland, then out onto a scenic trail high above the lake. In early summer, bluebells and flowering

The path above Lough Dan on the eastern base of Kanturk.

A stile on the ascent to Kanturk, with Knocknacloghoge behind.

gorse line the path. The path ends at a track after 1km; cross the track and climb a set of wooden steps on the opposite side, with another notice confirming that you are still on the route to Kanturk.

Climb to a stile beside a large boulder, where you cross the boundary into Wicklow Mountains National Park. Continue to follow the well-defined path as it climbs gradually along the shoulder ahead. The grassy trail leads easily through the heather, and there are fine views north across the sickle-shaped beach at the northwestern end of Lough Dan to the steep cliffs binding the lower slopes of Knocknacloghoge.

Near the top of the shoulder, the first landmark is a large, oval boulder that sits in isolation on a low rock base – so incongruously placed that it must be a glacial erratic. From here the path veers south and weaves through a maze of granite outcrops, hummocks and boulder formations. Though the mountain has no defined high point, this labyrinth of features makes it one of Wicklow's more memorable summits. You may find yourself grateful for the guidance of the path beneath your feet.

As you exit the maze, you are met by clear views ahead to Scarr. In wet conditions you will have to negotiate the occasional boggy patch as the path dips across a shallow hollow, then makes a gradual ascent to point 561m. The peaks to the south are now most engaging, with massive Tonelagee dominating the scene just across the Glenmacnass valley. The building on the skyline to its left is part of the summit reservoir that crowns Turlough Hill.

Continue southeast across the col, then begin the final ascent to Scarr, which means 'sharp rock'. Along the way you pass a small granite standing stone, and enjoy a bird's-eye view over Glenmacnass Waterfall. A final, steep climb brings you to the top of the mountain. The summit ridge is enjoyably narrow, with its edges defined by outcrops of mica-schist rock. The high point is marked by a small cairn – the first of the route – and fabulous 360° views that include the coastline as well as many of southern Wicklow's highest peaks.

Cross straight over the summit ridge and descend south along a broad shoulder, heading towards the right-hand corner of a small patch of forestry. The path is clear throughout and offers easy passage all the way. You arrive at the forest at a fence corner, with a rusty gate straight ahead. Turn left here and follow a rough vehicle track along the edge of the plantation. Within a few hundred metres you reach the forest's northeastern corner. Turn right here and begin to descend along the track, still keeping the trees to your right.

At the bottom of the plantation you come to a junction of tracks. Keep straight ahead here, climbing across a stile beside a metal gate. You are now on the route of the Wicklow Way, and can follow the waymarks all the way back to Oldbridge. Essentially you descend along the track to reach a road, then turn left. Follow the road over several undulations to the junction at Oldbridge, where you should turn left. The lay-by is 300m away on the left.

The descent path along the southern shoulder of Scarr.

ROUTE 20:
The Devil's Glen

A short walk through a wooded gorge to reach a dramatic waterfall on the Vartry River.

Grade:	1
Time:	1½ hours
Distance:	5km (3 miles)
Ascent:	130m (430ft)
Map:	OSi 1:50,000 sheet 56, or EastWest Mapping 1:30,000 *Wicklow East*.

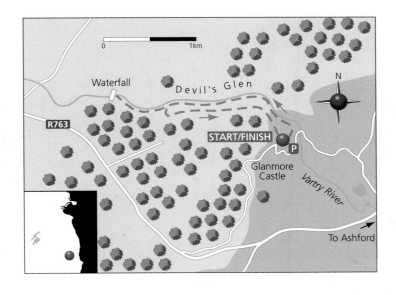

Start & Finish: The Devil's Glen parking area (grid ref: T247985). From Ashford, follow the R763 west for 3.5km. Where the road climbs steeply through a series of sharp bends, look out on the right for the entrance to the Devil's Glen. Follow this access road for almost 2km to reach a small parking area. The gates for the access road are locked every evening, and there is a board displaying the closing times.

The Devil's Glen is a popular woodland amenity area on the eastern edge of the Wicklow Mountains. This wild and secluded gorge is more than 100m deep, and thickly cloaked in a mixture of broadleaf and coniferous trees. Originally formed during the last Ice Age by meltwater draining from the high Wicklow glaciers, the glen now carries the rapids and falls of the Vartry River.

The Vartry itself rises beneath Great Sugar Loaf, some 18km away. In 1865 the river was damned near Roundwood, creating the Vartry Reservoir. This became the first clean water source for residents of Dublin city, most of whom had been drinking water from canals up to that point. Some 40 per cent of the capital's water still originates from the reservoir.

The area is owned and managed by Coillte, the state-owned forestry body. In 1994, the organisation instigated a policy entitled Sculpture In Woodland, commissioning a series of wooden sculptures from Irish and international artists. These works are located alongside the valley's trails, forming a natural, outdoor art gallery. Unfortunately a lack of maintenance means that some of the works have become overgrown, while others are beginning to fall into disrepair.

The valley contains a network of walking trails, with route information and a map displayed on a notice board near the entrance to the car park. The route described here visits the valley's natural highlights, though walkers who prefer a longer outing can easily extend the trip to include other parts of the glen. Note that the OS map does not portray the valley's paths accurately, and that some sections of the trail can be muddy after rain.

The Walk

Look for a path that begins in the corner of the car park opposite the access road. Follow this trail diagonally down and to the left, passing through an overarching tunnel of rhododendron. The path then drops down a steep wooded slope through a series of sharp switchbacks – follow the white arrows on wooden posts to stay on the correct route. The sound of the rapids on the Vartry River grow louder as you progress. Towards the bottom of the slope, keep left to reach the riverbank.

The Vartry River flows through the heart of the Devil's Glen.

Continue along the path, now climbing imperceptibly through birch and oak woodland. The path keeps very close to the river as it pours noisily through several boulder-strewn rapids, while the walls of the gorge close in on both sides. After perhaps thirty minutes you reach a junction where a broad track descends from the left to meet the riverside path. You will return to this track shortly, but for the moment continue straight ahead along the river. A few minutes later you climb a flight of stone steps and reach a lookout point just downstream of the Devil's Glen waterfall.

A rock arch on the path through the Devil's Glen.

The falls are impressive at any time of the year, but especially after long periods of rain. There is also a smaller but no less powerful cascade immediately below the main waterfall. The pool beneath the falls has been known to provide a refreshing swim during the summer months.

Return to the junction with the forestry track. Turn right here, climbing steeply through mature coniferous forest. Keep left at the next junction and follow a narrow path that contours along the southern rim of the glen, providing great views across the dense woodland canopy. Pass through an intriguing rock tunnel and stay on the main path to return to the parking area.

ROUTE 21:
Kilcoole Coastal Path

This linear route explores a stretch of low, gentle coastline with a return journey by train.

Grade:	1
Time:	3–4 hours
Distance:	14km (9 miles)
Ascent:	30m (100ft)
Map:	OSi 1:50,000 sheet 56, or EastWest Mapping 1:30,000 *Wicklow East*.

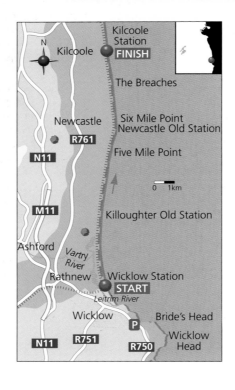

Start & Finish: The route starts at Wicklow train station (grid ref: T308948) and finishes at Kilcoole train station (grid ref: 0312079). Both stations are part of Irish Rail's intercity network, and have large adjacent car parks.

This route is a world away from the rugged mountain terrain normally associated with walking in Wicklow. It explores a stretch of coastline that is peaceful, gentle and unspoilt, and offers a perfect antidote for legs weary of trudging uphill. It provides a taste of the low coastline that characterises much of southern Wicklow, and along with the routes around Howth (see p. 11) and Bray Head (p. 20), it completes the picture in terms of the landscape that can be found along the region's seaboard.

This shoreline was shaped some 16,000 years ago at the end of the last Ice Age, when huge amounts of sand and gravel were deposited by retreating glaciers. Subsequent drifting movements created a coastal ridge some 4m high, which enclosed an area of low-lying inland marshes. Today this habitat is known as the Murrough Wetlands. The entire area is protected as a Special Area of Conservation and a Special Protection Area for birds. It is home to Ireland's largest colony of our rarest breeding bird, the Little Tern, with 50 to 100 adult pairs. A Little Tern Protection Scheme is mounted here from mid-May to mid-August each year. Peak season – and therefore one of the most impressive times to complete this route – is around the end of June.

This is a linear route between two train stations. Be sure to check train times before you head out because Kilcoole is a minor stop that has a commuter service from Monday to Saturday only, with trains heading towards Dublin in the morning and returning in the evening. This offers walkers a choice of either setting out from Wicklow around lunchtime and returning on the 5.30 p.m. service from Kilcoole, or catching the early train from Wicklow and reversing the route described.

Your choices will be widened if you have two vehicles at your disposal. In this case, consider adding a scenic extension to Wicklow Head at the southern end of the route. Instead of starting at Wicklow train station, begin from a car park just southeast of the town, beside the R750 in Bride's Glen (grid ref: T328932). From here, head down a path to the coast, then turn right along the coastal path. Follow this all the way around the cliffs to Wicklow Head, which is crowned by a former lighthouse built in the 1770s (now a private house). From here, retrace your steps north, then continue around the shore, past a golf course, to reach the mouldering ruins of Black Castle. Pass the town's picturesque harbour, and keep to the coast as much as possible through the town to rejoin the route described below. This extension will add 6km to your day's walk.

The coastal path between Kilcoole and Wicklow town.

The Walk

From Wicklow train station, head down the approach road for 100m. Turn left here onto a footpath signed 'River Walk and Nature Trail'. Follow the path to the bank of the Leitrim River, then cross a metal walkway attached to the railway bridge. Continue under a road bridge, then veer right along a road for 50m to bypass an enclave of houses. This is where you reach the coast, and there are fine, wide views that include Wicklow Harbour to the right and the Irish Sea ahead.

Turn left onto an earthen track above the shoreline. The pebble beach continues all the way to the end of the walk. The terrain at the top of the beach is grassy at first, with the pointed cones of Great Sugar Loaf and Little Sugar Loaf prominent on the horizon ahead.

The railway line is never far away on your left, and after 4km you pass a tiny white station. The building is marked 'Killoughter' and dated 1855, the year this section of the line was completed. The station was operational for just twelve years, however, being reduced to a level crossing ever since.

The path now narrows to a sandy trail that runs across low dunes and marram grass. On the left, fertile pastures lead to the eastern Wicklow Mountains. There are few signs of urban life and it seems very remote and peaceful. The dunes end at an Irish sign marking Five Mile Point, and the route continues across occasional rocks at the top of the breakwater. Follow a fence to reach another former station at Newcastle, which had an even shorter working lifespan and closed in 1964 after just nine years of operation.

The old railway station at Killoughter dates from 1855.

View inland across the Murrough Wetlands from the coastal path just south of Kilcoole.

At Newcastle the coast curves west slightly – this is your last chance to look back to Wicklow Head in the south. Continue past a small airstrip to reach Kilcoole Marshes, a tidal marsh just inland that provides an important habitat for several species of bird including Curlews, Redshanks and Little Egrets.

The outlet where the marsh drains into the sea is known as The Breaches, and is spanned by a metal railway bridge. You must walk close to the tracks here, so keep alert for oncoming trains. Pass through a pedestrian gate just before the bridge and turn left, walking along the gravel beside the tracks. Another gateway allows you to return to the beach on the northern bank of the river.

You now reach the stretch of shoreline that is used by Little Terns as a breeding ground. Access to the beach is restricted here between mid-May and mid-August to protect the eggs and chicks, which are well camouflaged and raised directly on the stones. If you are walking between these times you may well meet wardens from BirdWatch Ireland and the National Parks and Wildlife Service, who can provide binoculars and a wealth of fascinating information on the birds.

The path now re-enters an area of marram grass, and there are good views north to the Howth peninsula. Continue for the final 1.5km to Kilcoole train station. The beach in front of the station is sandy and popular with local visitors – a perfect place to rest while you await your train back to Wicklow.

Camaderry Circuit

A trip along
Glendalough's
Upper Lake leads to
fine views and an
enjoyable mountain-
top return.

Grade:	4
Time:	4–5 hours
Distance:	13km (8 miles)
Ascent:	630m (2,070ft)
Map:	OSi 1:50,000 sheet 56, EastWest Mapping 1:30,000 *Lugnaquilla & Glendalough*, or Harvey Superwalker 1:30,000 *Wicklow Mountains*.

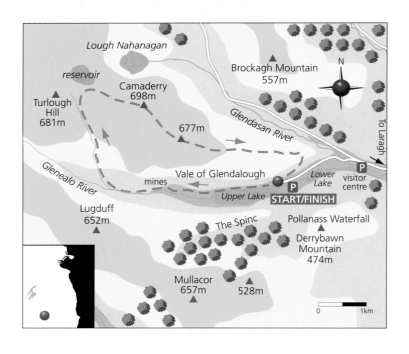

Start & Finish: Upper Lake car park at the end of the R757 in Glendalough, roughly 4km west of Laragh (grid ref: T111964). There is plenty of parking space here, and facilities include public toilets and a snack bar. There is a €4 charge to enter, however; have the exact change ready to pass through the automatic barrier. Alternatively, free parking is available 1.5km east at Glendalough Visitor Centre. From here, follow the green arrows along the path known as the Green Road to the Upper Lake car park.

T his enjoyable circuit is a tale of two halves. The outward part of the route follows the popular miner's track along Glendalough's Upper Lake. Depending on the time of the year, you may be appreciating the scenery in the company of throngs of tourists.

Once you pass the old mine workings at the western end of the lake, and especially once you are past the Glenealo footbridge of the Spinc Loop, the character of the route changes dramatically. From here you are suddenly alone amidst wild mountain terrain. There is a stream to guide you up the slope to Turlough Hill, but few signs of passing feet. As you make your way along Camaderry's summit ridge you join a well-defined path but the mountainous feeling continues, with fine 360° views encompassing most of Wicklow's highest peaks.

The wild atmosphere is enhanced by the wildlife, and this seems to be a particularly good route for spotting deer and feral goats.

It is worth mentioning the waterworks at the summit of Turlough Hill, which are visited on the route. This scheme became operational in 1974, and remains the only pumped-storage hydroelectricity plant in Ireland. It works by connecting an artificial summit reservoir with the natural corrie lake of Lough Nahanagan. Apart from the unnaturally flat-topped profile of the upper reservoir, scenic disruption is minor, and it is interesting to think of the power beneath your feet as you walk along the ridge beside the lakes.

The Walk

From the upper car park, head along the northern bank of Upper Lake. You have a choice of routes: either take the miner's road, a flat forest track that contours around 20m above the lake, or opt for the footpath along the lakeshore. If you take the miner's road, you will notice a stone cottage at the end of the tarmac, with a forest track coming down to its left. This is the track you will return along at the end of the route.

Ruins of a nineteenth-century mine building in the upper Glendalough valley.

Whichever way you progress along the lake, you will pass through a long stand of mature Scots pine. After roughly 500m there is a view to St Kevin's Bed on the opposite shore of the lake, the foundations of the church where St Kevin is said to be have been buried in the seventh century. The shoreline path climbs to join the miner's road near the western end of the lough, and you continue past the beach and marsh at the end of the lake.

The track now passes through an area littered with old mine paraphernalia – spoil heaps, rusted machinery and the remnants of several former mine buildings. The path becomes broken underfoot as it weaves its way through the ruins. When the Glenealo River floods it often inundates this area, sometimes destroying the path. Soon the trail consolidates again, climbing the valley headwall in a series of well-made switchbacks. The chutes and falls of the Glenealo are a constant companion during the ascent, and the section ends at a wooden footbridge across the river.

Walker on the track in the upper Glendalough valley.

Avoid the temptation to cross the river; you must leave the security of the path here, and strike out on your own across open mountain terrain. Continue ahead along the northern bank of the river. By doing this, you will find yourself naturally following a tributary stream that begins to arc northwest. Climb along this watercouse, with an intermittent, informal path through the grass and heather to reassure you.

Soon the flat-topped form of Turlough Hill Reservoir comes into sight ahead. This is your next goal. Climb steadily across the heather and rough grass, still picking a line just to the right of the stream. You will need to negotiate several wet patches before you emerge at the tall wire fence that encloses the mountaintop reservoir.

Turn right at the fence and join a well-worn path along its perimeter. At the southeastern corner of the fence, the path branches off and makes its

The route climbs beside a stream to reach flat-topped Turlough Hill.

way to the col beneath Camaderry. Follow the obvious trail, which leads a fairly direct line through the numerous peat hags that litter the col.

An easy climb then brings you up the rounded, grassy slope to the summit of Camaderry (698m), which has no real cairn except a couple of casual stones balanced atop a boulder. There are fine views across the valley to the north to Tonelagee and Mullaghcleevaun, while the brooding bulk of Lugnaquilla lies to the southwest.

Winter view of Tonelagee and Mullaghcleevaun from the 698m summit of Camaderry.

Descend southeast from the summit along the obvious path, climbing only slightly to pass over point 677m at the eastern edge of the ridge. This is where the real descent starts. Continue to follow the path southeast, dropping steeply at first and negotiating more wet patches. The angle eases as you progress, and the peat eventually gives way to a grassy trail though an expanse of bracken.

Follow the path down into trees, where you join the end of a forest track. Turn left and follow the track through several switchbacks until a waymarking post indicates you have joined a national park trail marked by silver arrows. Turn right here and follow the marked trail along the track. You contour across the hillside for a while before descending again and rejoining the miner's road near the stone cottage. Turn left onto the miner's road and walk the final 300m back to the car park.

Sika deer in the upper Glendalough valley.

Feb 2020 - very good again
old blue route
March 19
very good
very busy

ROUTE 23:
The Spinc Loop

An airy cliff-top path is the highlight of this wonderfully scenic circumnavigation of Glendalough's Upper Lake.

Grade:	3
Time:	3½–4 hours
Distance:	11.5km (7 miles)
Ascent:	400m (1,310ft)
Map:	OSi 1:50,000 sheet 56, EastWest Mapping 1:30,000 *Lugnaquilla & Glendalough*, or Harvey Superwalker 1:30,000 *Wicklow Mountains*.

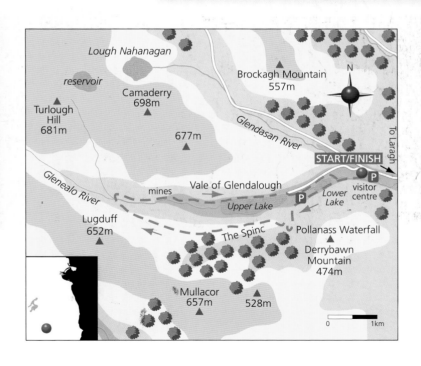

Start & Finish: The car park for the Glendalough Visitor Centre (grid ref: T126968) on the R757 road, roughly 3km west of Laragh. (Alternatively, you could save 3km walking by starting at the Upper Lake car park at the end of the road in Glendalough. This option costs €4; have the exact change ready for the automatic barrier. From the car park, follow signs to the park information office at the southeastern corner of the lake, where you join the route described below.)

O f the nine waymarked walking trails in the Glendalough valley, this route is the most popular. It climbs to the top of a long cliff on the southern side of the Upper Lake, where the exposure and the views are breathtaking. The route is fully signed and follows maintained paths throughout, making it suitable for fit leisure walkers.

The route then descends to the upper Glenealo valley and passes through the remains of an old mining settlement. Add a visit to Glendalough's monastic settlement or visitor centre at the beginning or end of the walk, and you have not just an immensely scenic route, but a historically interesting one too. What more could you want from a day out?

Finally, a note of warning: though the paths and signposts make this route accessible to a wide range of people, the route crosses open mountain terrain and all the normal rules of mountain walking apply. Bring warm clothing and avoid walking in poor visibility. The path also passes along the top of precipitous cliffs, and the utmost care is needed near the edge.

The Walk

Start from the footbridge at the southwestern corner of the visitor centre car park. There is a walk information board and the first of numerous waymarking posts. The Spinc Loop is signed throughout by the white arrows.

Cross the footbridge, then turn right along the wide path known as the Green Road. After 200m you come to a footbridge on the right, which provides access to the monastic city founded by St Kevin in the sixth century. The site includes Early Christian crosses, a 30m-high round tower and several churches and monastic dwellings.

Walk waymarking post in Lugduff Forest. The Spinc Loop is signed throughout by white arrows.

View over Glendalough's Upper and Lower Lakes from the cliffs of The Spinc.

When you are ready, return to the Green Road and follow it for over a kilometre, passing mature oak woodland beside the Lower Lake.

Before long you arrive at the park information office, housed in a small white cottage at the southeastern corner of Upper Lake. Around 20m beyond the office, turn left up a path signed for Pollanass Waterfall. All junctions are signed, so just keep following the white arrows to stay on the correct route.

Climb a series of steps beside the falls, which drop steeply though a narrow channel carved from the rock. At the top of the path turn left onto a forest track, then quickly right onto another track. A hundred metres past the second junction, the route is signed to the right. Here you leave the track and begin a steep ascent up a long flight of steps made from old railway sleepers. Pine trees are planted densely on all sides.

It comes as something of a relief to exit the trees, both to escape the claustrophobia of the boughs and because the ground now flattens out underfoot. Just a few metres further on you reap the reward for your effort – the first magnificent view over Glendalough Upper Lake. The airy vantage point is simply spectacular, and the view will stay with you for the next kilometre as you traverse along the top of the cliffs some 200m above the water.

Most of the path along the cliffs is constructed from wooden sleepers, so it is a simple matter to follow the route forward. There is a good view too over the path that zigzags down to the lake from upper Glenealo valley. This is where you are heading next.

At the western end of the lake the sleepers split at a junction. Keep right, climbing to the highest point of the route at just over 500m. The path now begins to descend, dropping gently to a footbridge over the Glenealo River. Keep an eye open here for deer.

Cross the bridge and turn right, following the path alongside the

Crossing a footbridge over the Glenealo River in the upper Glendalough valley.

chutes and falls of the river. Ahead is a fine view along the length of the Glendalough valley, with the lake still far below. A series of well-made switchbacks helps you down the valley headwall, depositing you at the old mining settlement. Here you pass a variety of old mine paraphernalia – spoil heaps, rusted machinery and the remnants of several former mine buildings. The path becomes broken underfoot as it weaves its way through the ruins. When the Glenealo River floods it often inundates this area, sometimes destroying the path.

Continue downstream, passing a marsh and a wide sandy beach, to reach the western end of Upper Lake. The wide gravel track known as the miner's road now contours ahead, keeping around 20m above the lake. If you want to get closer to the water's edge, watch out for a small footpath that descends to the lakeshore after roughly 300m.

Whichever way you choose, you will pass through a long stand of mature Scots pine, home to red squirrels and Long-eared Owls. A kilometre from the start of the lake, there is a view across the water to the foundations of the church where St Kevin is said to be have been buried in the seventh century.

The shoreline path and the miner's road both deposit you at the car park at the eastern end of the lough. Now cross the left side of the car park and join the end of a wooden boardwalk. This carries you easily past Lower Lake, and brings you to a junction with the Green Road just before the monastic city. Turn left here and complete the final 400m back to the visitor centre car park.

Mullacor Circuit

Traverse the cliffs high above Glendalough's Upper Lake, then climb across the peaks that enclose the valley to the south.

Grade:	4
Time:	4–5 hours
Distance:	11.5km (7 miles)
Ascent:	640m (2,100ft)
Map:	OSi 1:50,000 sheet 56, EastWest Mapping 1:30,000 *Lugnaquilla & Glendalough*, or Harvey Superwalker 1:30,000 *Wicklow Mountains*.

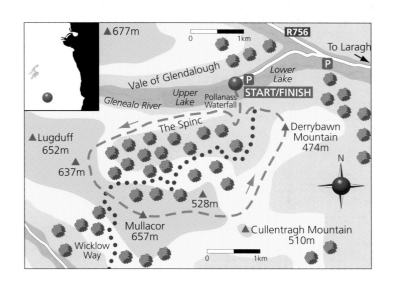

Start & Finish: Upper Lake car park at the end of the R757 in Glendalough, roughly 4km west of Laragh (grid ref: T111964). There is plenty of parking space here, and facilities include public toilets and a snack bar. There is a €4 charge to enter, however; have the exact change ready to pass through the automatic barrier. Alternatively, free parking is available 1.5km east at Glendalough Visitor Centre. From here, follow the green arrows along the path known as the Green Road to the park information office, where you join the route described.

This route explores the ridge between Glendalough and Glenmalure, probably the two most renowned valleys in the Wicklow Mountains. The mountains themselves have rounded, peat-covered slopes and are not overly challenging, but provide fine views.

The route starts by traversing the cliffs of The Spinc (see p. 105). This lofty path allows fantastic views over Glendalough Upper Lake. The route then veers away from Glendalough, embarking on a mountain circuit that has its high point at the 657m summit of Mullacor. From here, mighty Lugnaquilla seems just a stone's throw away to the southwest. The pleasantly narrow ridge of Derrybawn provides an enjoyable finale before a steep descent brings you back into Lugduff Forest.

Footpaths and sections of boardwalk ease your progress for most of the route, and waymarks are followed as far as the col between Lugduff and Mullacor. From here you are on your own in terms of navigation, though there are still informal paths to guide you on the ground.

If you have never explored Glendalough's monastic settlement or visitor centre, you might also want to consider using the alternative start/finish point. This adds 3km to the walk, but is well worth it in terms of the historic insight into life in Glendalough going back to the sixth century AD.

The Walk

From the Upper Lake car park, follow signs to the park information office, which is housed in a small white cottage at the southeastern corner of the lake. Turn right just past the office and continue for 20m, then turn left up a path signed for Pollanass Waterfall. There are frequent waymarking posts during the first part of the route, and you should begin by following the white and the red arrows.

Climb a series of steps beside the falls, which drop steeply though a narrow channel carved from the rock. At the top of this path turn left onto a forest track, then quickly right onto another track. All junctions are signed; just keep following the white or red arrows to stay on the correct route. A hundred metres past the second junction, the route is signed to the right. Here you leave the track and begin a steep ascent up a long flight of steps made from old railway sleepers. Pine trees are planted densely on

The path along Lugduff mountain, above Glendalough.

all sides, and the effect is of a dark escalator forging a way upward within an oppressive green cavern.

It comes as something of a relief to exit the trees, both to escape the claustrophobia of the boughs, and because the ground now flattens out underfoot. Just a few metres further on you are rewarded with your first magnificent view over Glendalough Upper Lake. The spectacular view will stay with you for the next kilometre as you traverse along the top of the cliffs some 200m above the lake.

Most of the path along the cliffs is constructed from wooden sleepers, so it is a simple matter to follow the route. At the western end of the lake, just beyond another fantastic viewpoint, you come to a junction. The white Spinc Loop continues ahead, but this route turns left, now following just the red arrows.

The path veers southwest away from the lake, following the edge of the forest towards Lugduff. Soon the trees are left behind, and you are out on the open, tussock-covered slopes that make up most of the high ground of the route. The path remains obvious underfoot and after a short climb you sweep left, avoiding Lugduff summit and arriving instead at the col between Lugduff and Mullacor.

Here you meet the boardwalk of the Wicklow Way, which crosses the col on its way to Glenmalure. Cross straight over the sleepers and continue

A section of boardwalk carries you across bog pools beneath Lugduff mountain.

ahead on a peaty path that climbs the broad slope towards Mullacor. You have now left all the signed routes behind, and must rely on your own navigational skills.

The ground is occasionally boggy underfoot as you make your way to Mullacor, a wide summit marked first by a small stone cairn, then by a diminutive wooden post. There are great views southwest across Glenmalure to Lugnaquilla, while the Derrybawn ridge – your next goal – can be clearly seen to the east.

A long, gradual descent now brings you to a fence corner. Cross the stile and follow the fence ahead for 500m. A national park post now marks a path junction. Turn sharp left here, leaving the fence and following a peat path towards the Derrybawn ridge. The narrow ridge provides good views, and the terrain varies between wet peat and rock underfoot. A gradual, undulating climb brings you to the northern tip of the ridge, where a small cairn marks the summit.

Continue north for another 50m, then veer left onto an eroded path that drops steeply off the western flank of the mountain. Pick your way carefully down the slope to meet the forest below. Cross straight over the first forest road, continuing to descend along another steep section of path on the other side. At the second forest road, turn left. Within 300m you arrive at a junction of tracks that you should recognise from your outward journey. Turn right here, following a sign to the car park. A hundred metres further on, turn right onto the path beside Pollanass Waterfall. This brings you back down beside the cascade, and deposits you back beside the park information office.

On the Derrybawn ridge, approaching the final summit of the route.

Vale of Clara

Follow a signed walking circuit through pristine native woodland on the banks of the Avonmore River.

Grade:	2
Time:	2½–3 hours
Distance:	9.5km (6 miles)
Ascent:	100m (330ft)
Map:	OSi 1:50,000 sheet 56

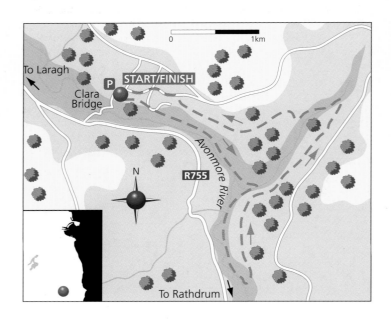

Start & Finish: A forest entrance in the Vale of Clara (grid ref: T171923). Access is via the R755 Laragh–Rathdrum road. Around 6km from Laragh or 5km from Rathdrum, turn north off the R755 onto a minor road signed to Clara Vale RC Church. Descend a steep hill and take care across a narrow, single-file bridge at the bottom. Pass the church and continue up the other side, arriving at a forest entrance on the right around 250m later. The entrance is marked Vale of Clara Nature Reserve, and has parking space for around six vehicles.

Most Irish walkers are familiar with the country's sad history of deforestation. Neolithic farmers dealt the first blow to Ireland's extensive woodlands when they began clearing trees for fields in 3000 BC. The process of felling continued, with another major onslaught in the seventeenth and eighteenth centuries. By 1800 Ireland was the least forested country in Europe. In the last few decades, numerous non-native conifer plantations have been cultivated, bringing the country's total forest coverage up to 10 per cent. Yet just 1 per cent of Ireland's surface area is natural, broadleaf woodland. Little wonder that the pockets of native trees are highly prized, and often protected within conservation areas.

The Vale of Clara Nature Reserve protects one of the most extensive sessile oak woodlands in Ireland. Though the area was inter-planted with commercial conifers in the second half of the 1900s, these species are now being removed to allow the native plants to flourish. Today, walkers can delight in a large area of mature oak trees, interspersed with other deciduous species like birch, hazel, rowan and holly. Add the presence of the meandering Avonmore River, and you have a beautiful, peaceful environment that seems a million miles from the hustle and bustle of modern life. Spring and autumn are particularly pretty times to visit.

The woodland has three signed walking circuits, 2km, 5.6km and 9.5km long. Here we describe the longest route, which is fully waymarked with blue arrows. It follows paths and tracks throughout and has some gentle climbs but nothing too strenuous. Suitable for all the family.

The Walk

Begin by following the track away from the entrance gate. Immediately you are surrounded by mature, broadleaf trees, and following a leafy track underfoot.

All the routes in the Vale of Clara are clearly signed. This circuit follows the blue arrows.

On the forest track near the start of the Vale of Clara looped walk.

This sets the scene for the rest of the walk, most of which will be spent on similar terrain.

Around 100m from the entrance you come to a junction, with the blue route signed both straight ahead and to the left. Keep straight ahead for now, and you will return from the left at the end of the circuit.

It is not long before the red and the green routes branch off, and with the blue route forging ahead on its own. After a kilometre of walking through beautiful birch, oak and hazel trees, the path draws close to the Avonmore River. A little further on there is a chance to step down onto the water's edge, at a confluence where a stream comes in from the left. It is a lovely spot, and along with a couple of waterside benches a little further on, makes a great place for a break.

The path veers left along the banks of the tributary, which is crossed via a wooden footbridge. You then return to the Avonmore, which is followed for a further kilometre. Enclaves of silver-trunked birch are interspersed by majestic stands of mature oak, giving an effect of lush variety and fertility.

The route is eventually signed left, away from the riverbank. You now begin a gradual ascent to a point around 80m above the valley floor, where you begin to contour around the hillside. On the way the route passes through several junctions, each of which is clearly signed. You are surrounded all the while by native trees, but where the branches thin there are great views west to the summit of mighty Lugnaquilla.

The Avonmore River is a central feature of the walk.

At the northeastern corner of the reserve the route begins to descend, then swings sharp left. Watch out now for a post directing you right, off the main track and across another wooden footbridge. Follow the signs through two more track junctions, passing through more impressive oak woodland.

Roughly 2km beyond the footbridge you emerge from the trees and join a narrow road. Turn left here and follow the tarmac downhill for around 400m. The route now diverts left, re-entering the woodland on a narrow footpath. A short, final descent through the trees brings you back to the junction you passed at the start of the walk. Turn right here to return to the entrance gateway.

Lugnaquilla:
An Overview

L ugnaquilla is a mountain of superlatives, with a wide range of accolades to describe it. At 925m high, it is Ireland's thirteenth highest mountain. It is the highest point in the country outside County Kerry, and the highest summit in the province of Leinster. It is over 100m higher than the next tallest mountain in Wicklow, and the only Munro (mountain over 3,000ft) in the county. No wonder it is seen as a hillwalking test piece, and has a magnetic force that draws serious walkers back again and again to explore it from different angles.

On a clear day from the summit views encompass much of Wicklow, South Leinster and even Wales. The summit itself is a flat, grassy plateau, but its flanks are cut by three glacial corries. A short distance northwest of the summit is the North Prison, to the northeast Fraughan Rock Glen, while to the southeast lies the South Prison. All these corries have their own distinct character, and in this book we describe three different routes that approach the peak along each corrie. These are the three most popular and varied routes from a large number of established options – in total there are at least twelve different ascent and descent routes to and from Lugnaquilla, which radiate around the summit like the spokes of a wheel. The other main options are summarised in the closest route description.

The mountain is such a focal point, and invites approach from so many directions, that many local walkers manage to establish quite a relationship with it, and refer to fondly it as 'Lug'. Despite such familiarity, this is not a peak that can be taken lightly. Lugnaquilla is notorious for its bad weather, and the summit is covered by cloud five days out of seven. With so many corries around the summit, navigating in the mist is a serious challenge, and local mountain rescue teams attend incidents and fatalities on the mountain on a regular basis. Even if you are an experienced walker, the advice is to watch the forecast carefully and wait for good weather before you attempt the peak.

Beneath the cliffs of Lugnaquilla's South Prison.

Lugnaquilla from the Glen of Imaal

This long but immensely scenic circuit lets you explore the wider Lugnaquilla massif, and includes 5km of fine mountain-top walking.

Grade:	5
Time:	6½–7½ hours
Distance:	19km (12 miles)
Ascent:	920m (3,020ft)
Map:	OSi 1:50,000 sheet 56, EastWest Mapping 1:30,000 *Lugnaquilla & Glendalough*, or Harvey Superwalker 1:30,000 *Wicklow Mountains*.

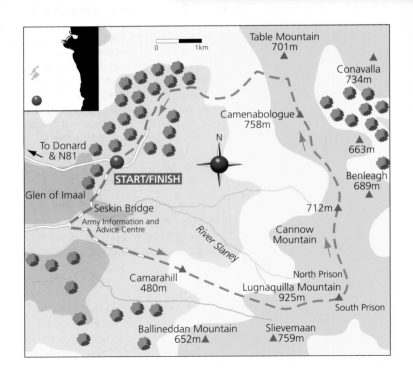

Start & Finish: A forest entrance in the northeastern corner of the Glen of Imaal (grid ref: S982948). Approach via the N81 Dublin–Blessington road. Around 17km south of Blessington, turn east towards Donard. In the village, turn left, then immediately right at a staggered crossroads. Continue straight ahead for 6km, and park beside a forest entrance on the left, opposite a sharp right bend in the road. There is parking space here for around four vehicles. If you need more space, continue along the route of the walk and park at Fenton's pub, just before the route turns left towards Camarahill.

The Glen of Imaal has long been a launch pad for ascents of Lugnaquilla. We will follow the most straightforward route to the summit, over Camarahill (known as the 'Tourist Route'), and then continue north to 758m-high Camenabologue, crossing 5km of fine upland terrain on the way.

One of the highlights is the dramatic view down the glacial corrie known as the North Prison. The word Lugnaquilla translates from the Irish *Log na Coille* as 'Hollow of the Wood'. The North Prison is most likely to be the hollow referred to because from a distance it is the most striking of Lugnaquilla's three coums.

This is a long mountain route and there are several hazards to be aware of. First are the natural dangers that surround Lugnaquilla's summit plateau. The cliffs that bind the North and South Prisons are particularly steep, and solid navigational skills are required to cross this area in poor visibility. This route also involves its own particular, unnatural danger as it crosses the Irish army's artillery range. Access is completely forbidden on days of scheduled firing, and on all other days there are just two approved walking routes through the area, both of which we use in this route: the first for the ascent up Camarahill, and the second for the descent from Camenabologue through the forest.

As well as checking the weather forecast before you head out you must also check the army's firing schedule: look for the monthly Glen of Imaal notices in the news section of Mountaineering Ireland's website, www.mountaineering.ie, call the artillery range's Warden Service on Tel: 045 404 653, or visit the Army Information Centre near the start of this walk. Firing schedules are also posted at many of the key access points within the area itself, and red flags fly around the perimeter of the range on firing days.

You should not deviate from the approved trails as there may be unexploded shells and other military debris lying off the path. If firing is taking place and you are still keen to complete the route, consider approaching it from Glenmalure instead. Follow the route described on p. 125 to reach the top of Lugnaquilla via Fraughan Rock Glen. Then follow the route described here as far as the col beneath Table Mountain. Instead of turning left here, turn right and descend for 5km back to the car park at the head of Glenmalure, always following the track that keeps closest to the southern side of the Avonbeg River.

The Walk

From the forest entrance, follow the road southwest for 1.5km. Cross the bridge over the River Slaney, then pass the army information office and Fenton's pub. Just past the pub, turn left onto a lane, which soon dwindles to a track. After 400m, veer right, then continue straight ahead to reach a track crossroads almost 1km later.

Cross straight over this junction and begin to climb in earnest; there are still some 700m of vertical ascent separating you from the summit. The route is obvious, following a clear path straight along the middle of the rounded, peaty shoulder that rises ahead of you. Camarahill is more of a point on the ridge rather than a peak in its own right, but it does mark a brief respite in the angle of ascent.

The climb is steady until you reach the steeper, rock-strewn slope that guards the summit itself. A final effort here will bring you to the wide expanse of cropped grass that adorns the summit plateau, which is known as Percy's Table, named in honour of Colonel Percy, an eighteenth-century landowner from the Glen of Imaal.

Looking along the North Prison from Lugnaquilla's summit plateau.

In good visibility you may want to divert north once you have reached the plateau, to enjoy fine views from the top of the cliffs of the North Prison. Otherwise, continue directly to the official summit in the middle of the plateau. As you reach the trig point and huge stone cairn that mark the highest point in Wicklow, the views open up to the east.

The next 5km of the route trace the edge of the artillery range. Regular metal warning signs mark the range boundary; make sure to keep these on your left to avoid straying into forbidden (and potentially explosive) territory.

From the summit, begin by heading northeast across the plateau. In clear weather you might want to keep further west here, for more good views along the North Prison. Then head over to the eastern edge of the shoulder above Fraughan Rock Glen. Pick up a path that heads north along the shoulder; following this trail will ensure you avoid the pitfall of veering too far west along Cannow Mountain.

Descend easily along the path, with the rock-strewn hummock of point

Warning signs mark the boundary of Glen of Imaal Artillery Range.

View across Benleagh and Camenabologue from the northern slopes of Lugnaquilla.

712m and the rounded dome of Camenabologue clearly visible ahead. Cross a shallow col then continue over point 712m, with Benleagh's maze of peat hags off to your right. This is a delightful stretch of walking across firm, rock-studded terrain, and with extensive views northeast to Tonelagee and Turlough Hill.

As you continue to follow the path north, the ground turns to peat underfoot. There are occasional wet patches as you undulate across several hummocks, then begin the final ascent up the southern slopes of Camenabologue. A large stone cairn marks the 758m-high summit (the first cairn of the route since Lugnaquilla). The vantage point reveals a 360° panorama of the Blessington Lakes to the north, the Glen of Imaal to the west and Lugnaquilla to the south.

Continue north from Camenabologue, descending easily through a scatter of peat hags to reach the col beneath Table Mountain, the saddle that separates Glenmalure from the Glen of Imaal. It is marked by a grassy track and a Defence Force map board. Turn left onto the track then, 20m later, veer left onto a side path. You are now descending back into the upper reaches of the Glen of Imaal. Follow the trail to a gate, where you will see more army signs. From here, follow the signed path, as it is the only approved descent route on this side of the artillery range.

Turn right at the gate and descend steeply. Continue across two bridges to reach a forest track, which you follow downhill for roughly 2km. Army arrows then direct you off to the right, and you follow a side track for the final 500m before arriving back at the forest entrance where the route began.

Lugnaquilla dominates the head of the Glen of Imaal.

ROUTE 27:

Lugnaquilla from Glenmalure

Probably the most scenic circuit over Lugnaquilla, this compact route includes visits to beautiful Art's Lough and dramatic Fraughan Rock Glen.

Grade:	5
Time:	5–6 hours
Distance:	13km (8 miles)
Ascent:	800m (2,620ft)
Map:	OSi 1:50,000 sheet 56, EastWest Mapping 1:30,000 *Lugnaquilla & Glendalough*, or Harvey Superwalker 1:30,000 *Wicklow Mountains*.

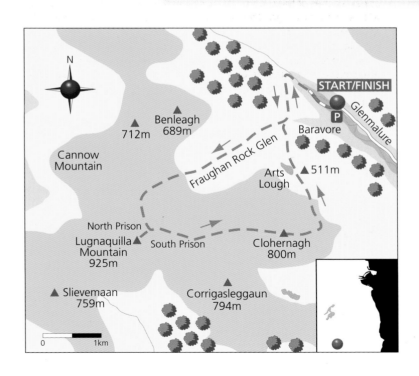

Start & Finish: A large car park at Baravore, at the head of Glenmalure (grid ref: T066942). Glenmalure is generally reached via the Military Road from Laragh.

This is my favourite approach to Lugnaquilla. The terrain and the scenery are both dramatic and varied, and the circuit is conveniently compact. The route starts and finishes in the cliff-fringed valley of Fraughan Rock Glen, and passes over 800m-high Cloghernagh as well as the summit of Lugnaquilla. The jewel in the crown is the high, secluded lake of Arts Lough, a hidden gem set amidst a wild landscape that is surely one of the region's most beautiful sights.

The trip is a lesson in glacial landscaping. The walk begins at the head of Glenmalure, the longest glacial valley in Ireland, and every topographical feature on the route owes its form to the scouring movement of past ice sheets. Prominent landforms include the vertical walls of Fraughan Rock Glen and the hanging valley above, as well as the high-altitude hollow that holds Arts Lough.

There are also interesting origins behind many of the place names on the route. The name Glenmalure has several explanations, but the most evocative stems from the Irish *Gleann Maoil Ura*, meaning 'Valley of the Invigorating Hill'. The name Fraughan Rock Glen refers to the *fraochán* plant, or bilberry, whose fruit is traditionally gathered on Fraughan Sunday, the last Sunday in July. Finally there is Art's Lough, which was named in Famine times in memory of a man who died after eating an eel from its waters.

As well as the route described, there is the option of an alternative descent to bring you out 3km further south along the Glenmalure road (grid ref: T087921). This is a handy option for walkers staying overnight at The Glenmalure Lodge. From the summit of Cloghernagh, head east onto the path described below. Instead of turning north onto the ramp to Art's Lough, continue straight ahead, following the path along the edge of the cliffs that define the northern edge of the shoulder. The path carries you down to The Zigzags, a track that switchbacks down the base of the shoulder. Continue past the dramatic Carrawaystick Waterfall to finish at the bridge over the Avonbeg River.

Finally, a word of warning: this is a challenging route across a high, remote mountain, and there are several stretches with no path. As well as taking care to avoid the corries around the summit of Lugnaquilla, you will need to pay particular attention to navigation on the descent from Cloghernagh to Fraughan Rock Glen. The paths here are most accurately displayed on the EastWest Mapping sheet, but enough hazards remain that the route is best avoided in poor visibility.

The Walk

From the car park, walk towards the ford across the Avonbeg River. Turn right in front of the river and join a footpath that heads upstream for 100m, then cross the river via a footbridge. On the opposite bank, turn right onto a vehicle track. Continue past the building of the Glenmalure Youth Hostel, then turn left at a track junction.

The track leads steadily uphill through the forest, then out into the more open surrounds of Fraughan Rock Glen. The Benleagh cliffs tower overhead on your right, and a waterfall plunges down the valley headwall. There is a forestry plantation on the southern side of the valley; you will descend along the western edge of these trees at the end of the circuit.

For now, follow the track to the base of the waterfall, then climb steeply up the right-hand side of the falls. As you pass over the lip of the headwall into the hanging valley above, the landscape is suddenly much wilder and more rugged, with a flat basin backed by the steep ridge that drops down from Lugnaquilla's summit plateau.

Keep following the bank of the main stream to the top of another rise. Cross a boggy hollow, then climb straight up the headwall. You can choose your line of ascent depending on how steep you want the climb to be – the slope is steepest to the south and tapers off to the north. The ground underfoot is punctuated by numerous small hummocks, which are covered by tussock grass and studded with rock outcrops. Pick your line through the obstacles and climb steeply to the ridgeline, where the rough ground is instantly replaced by a gentle slope of close-cropped grass, which provides a perfect walking surface across the entire summit plateau.

The track through Fraughan Rock Glen, with the Benleagh cliffs overhead.

127

A cairn and trig point mark the 925m summit of Lugnaquilla.

Turn left when you reach the top of the ridge, and soon the prominent summit cairn will come into view to the south. Walk diagonally across the plateau to reach it, taking care to avoid steep ground at the top of the North Prison. Lugnaquilla's trig point sits atop a massive circular plinth and there are predictably fine 360° views, and a nearby orientation plaque indicates the direction of surrounding landmarks.

Your next goal is Cloghernagh, but care is needed to reach this peak safely. The steep corrie of the South Prison intrudes on the direct line of approach, so you will sweep northeast around the rim of the corrie before you can straighten up and head east along the broad ridge to Cloghernagh. A wide path along the top of the shoulder makes for easy progress; look south as you near Cloghernagh for a great view over Kelly's Lough. The 800m summit itself is distinguished by a small cairn, and expansive views to the east.

Take care now to locate the correct descent route to Art's Lough, which is hidden from view below. Your aim is to reach a ramp that descends north towards the lake. From Cloghernagh, follow a faint path that descends east for 200m, then veers northeast to reach the top of the cliffs on the northern edge of the shoulder (this trail is marked more clearly on the EastWest Mapping and Harvey maps.) At the western corner of the cliffs, turn left onto another narrow path that is marked by occasional cairns of white stone.

This path traverses north along the top of the drop, then descends. A short distance later Art's Lough comes into view below, at the foot of steep cliffs on Cloghernagh's northeastern face. Follow the path down the ramp towards the lough, passing several large rocks.

The shore of beautiful Art's Lough, on the northeastern slopes of Cloghernagh.

The ramp carries you almost all the way to the lake, though you will have to make a short detour through the heather if you want to reach the water's edge. You will now see a wire fence that runs parallel to the lake, just above its eastern shore. Follow this fence north to a corner, then turn right, following a boggy path along the left side of the fence. Descend steeply alongside a forestry plantation, heading back towards Fraughan Rock Glen.

Towards the bottom of the slope, veer left slightly and pass through a gate around 150m west of the forest. Now follow a rough track to the river, which is easily forded in normal water conditions. Continue up the opposite bank to join the main track through the glen. Turn right here and retrace your initial steps back to the start.

ROUTE 28:

Lugnaquilla via the South Prison

A long forest approach brings you to a dramatic circuit that cuts right through the heart of the South Prison.

Grade:	5
Time:	5–6 hours
Distance:	16km (10 miles)
Ascent:	735m (2,410ft)
Map:	OSi 1:50,000 sheet 56, EastWest Mapping 1:30,000 *Lugnaquilla & Glendalough*, or Harvey Superwalker 1:30,000 *Wicklow Mountains*.

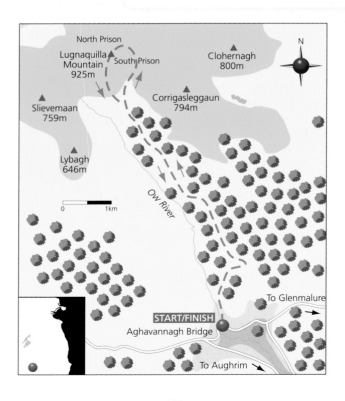

130

Start & Finish: Aghavannagh Bridge (grid ref: T056861), which can be reached via either a minor road from Aughrim or the Military Road from Laragh and Glenmalure. There is room to park two or three cars at the entrance to the forestry track at the eastern end of the bridge. Park tight to the left side of the entrance and be careful not to cause an obstruction as the track is used by forestry vehicles.

Of the three routes up Lugnaquilla described in this book, this is the least known and least frequented. It is an outing of two halves: a long approach along forest tracks, followed by a steep and rewarding circuit around the cliff-fringed basin of the South Prison. This captivating corrie is both daunting and majestic, the soaring rockfaces providing a fitting home to raptors such as the peregrine falcon.

The route starts and finishes at Aghavannagh which is so remote it has been described as 'the last place God made'. Aghavannagh is the southern terminus of the Military Road, which crosses the heart of the Wicklow Mountains and finishes some 70km north in Rathfarnham, County Dublin. The road was built between 1800 and 1809 to give the British army access to the mountains and help it control the remaining rebels from the 1798 uprising. Four military barracks were located along the road, with the last one sited in Aghavannagh.

The route itself starts and finishes along forest tracks, with 12km of track walking in total. Many walkers find such long stretches of forestry rather wearisome, but you can reduce the burden by copying the approach of Scottish walkers and use a mountain bike to cover the lower stretches. By cycling to the end of the track, you are left with a compact hiking circuit around 4km long, and the whole outing should take just 3½ hours.

If you decide to complete the route by foot, and if water levels are not too high, you may prefer to vary the descent route slightly. After completing the circuit of the South Prison, return to the forest but do not cross the stile. Instead, head south between the stream and the edge of the forest. At the confluence with the stream that flows down between Slievemaan and Lugnaquilla, cross to the western bank. About 500m later you come to a beautiful waterfall where the river plunges over a rocky lip into a sheer gorge below. Continue carefully past the ravine then recross the river, still descending beside the forest until you reach a point at grid reference T042890. Here, cross an old stile on the left and join the end of another forest track, which carries you straight ahead for the final 3km back to Aghavannagh Bridge.

The Walk

From Aghavannagh Bridge, walk north along the forestry track for a few hundred metres to a fork. Turn right here and climb steadily through the

The cliffs of Lugnaquilla's South Prison.

trees to another junction. Turn left here and continue to climb straight ahead for another 4km until you reach a turning circle at the end of the track. (Note that the junction shown on the OSi map about 1.5km before the end of the track no longer exists.)

Cross a stile over the boundary fence of the forest. You are now out onto open mountain terrain. Drop down a short slope and cross the stream, the nascent Ow River, which drains the South Prison. This is a good place to study the southern shoulder of Lugnaquilla, which you will be descending later in the route. It is also a good idea to make a mental note of this part of the forest so you can find it again on the return leg.

Climb steadily along the western side of the stream, following a faint and intermittent path. The brooding cliffs of the South Prison now loom directly ahead. As the ground begins to flatten out, cross to the eastern bank of the stream and continue north into the heart of the corrie. You will notice a conspicuous gully cleaving through the cliffs on your left. This is the South Prison's Central Gully – it stretches for 300 vertical metres and includes one particularly high step over a chockstone. Passage up the gully is possible in dry conditions, but it is a committed scramble and suitable only for those with previous experience across technical ground.

For the vast majority of walkers, the best way of 'escaping the prison' is to follow the broad, grassy tongue known as Green Street. This is a fantastic

At the highest point in Wicklow: the 925m summit of Lugnaquilla.

way to reach the top of Lugnaquilla, but if it looks too abrupt for your liking, you can avoid any steep ground by heading east and then northeast onto the mountain's eastern shoulder.

There are numerous route options as you progress along Green Street, but the line of least resistance is always obvious. Climb steeply up the grassy slope to reach a flatter area under some slab-covered cliffs. Now turn northwest and climb the steep slope above, weaving around patches of scree and outcrops of rock. The gradient is physically demanding, but the ground is never dangerous underfoot, except in winter conditions.

At the top of the slope you emerge abruptly onto Lugnaquilla's summit plateau. After the confines of the corrie, the sudden expansion of space is impressive. The large summit cairn lies just a few hundred metres west across flat ground, and long views stretch away in every direction.

The descent from Lugnaquilla requires great care in poor visibility. If in doubt, follow the well-worn path that heads southwest along the

View of Lugnaquilla's South Prison from the upper Ow Valley.

boundary of the Glen Imaal Artillery Range, then veer east and descend to the col between Lugnaquilla and Slievemaan. From here you can contour east to return to the forest.

In good conditions, however, it is much more direct to descend south from the summit of Lugnaquilla, passing above the cliffs of the South Prison. As you reach flatter ground, veer southeast and negotiate a small boulder field before rejoining the stream that flows down the corrie. Descend a short way along the stream, then cross it to reach the stile at the end of the forest track. It is now a simple matter of reversing your outward journey to return to the start of the walk.

Descending towards Cloghernagh from Lugnaquilla.